I Would Follow

JESUS

I Would Follow

JESUS

❧

Writings from the Heart of
JOSEPH STOWELL

A TRIBUTE

I WOULD FOLLOW

JESUS

༄

Writings from the Heart of
JOSEPH STOWELL

A TRIBUTE

MOODY PUBLISHERS
CHICAGO

ISBN: 0-8024-5686-3

1 3 5 7 9 10 8 6 4 2

Printed in the United States of America

An Incurable Contagious Love for Jesus
A Tribute to
Dr. Joseph M. Stowell III

Wat will last forever? Pose that question to Dr. Joe Stowell and you will find somewhere in his answer *"the centrality of Jesus Christ."* You want proof for that statement? Trace his footsteps, replay his conversations, or review his writings . . . and you will find all the evidence you need that he is a Jesus lover.

There is something about the name Jesus he loves, adores, and has given his life to make known to people around the world. His love for Jesus has resulted in a zest for life that is attractive and contagious.

Simply stated, Joe Stowell is one of those special Christ-followers whose life gives powerful witness to the words of Jesus: "I came that they might have life, and might have it abundantly" (John 10:10).

Dr. Stowell's life is marked by his compelling combination of a love for Jesus, a gift for connecting with people, and a zest for life. There are no dull moments with Joe Stowell! And that is why you will enjoy reading this book, a collection of the "best of Stowell" that captures the essence of the man who has served Christ so effectively for so long.

You will see Jesus in the pages that follow. But because of his gift for connecting with people, you will also experience the warm insights—insights most of us would miss—from the intersection of his life with the lives of others who have also encountered the living Christ. And Joe Stowell's zest for life enlivens the application of truth from the pages of Scripture in creative and compelling ways. So take some time to savor and enjoy these words of truth from a master practitioner.

While this book contains the words of Dr. Joe Stowell, the project has been prepared without his knowledge. (Even a president as engaged in hands-on leadership as Dr. Stowell doesn't always know everything taking place!) Indeed, this book is part of our campus-wide effort to say "thank you" to a man who has done so much for Moody Bible Institute and for the cause of Christ.

Sprinkled throughout this work are words of tribute from other Christian leaders who have come to know and love Joe Stowell as much as we do. They —along with the great people at Moody Publishers—have helped us fashion a work that we believe captures the heart and passion of Joe Stowell.

Joe, all of us at Moody love you, and we will miss you. You might be changing your place of ministry, but a part of your heart will always remain here.

For the Moody family,
DR. CHARLES DYER AND DR. LARRY MERCER

CONTENTS

Section 4

AM I A SOLDIER OF THE CROSS?

Section 5

BEAUTIFUL SAVIOR

Section 6

TRIBUTES

ONE

I NEED THEE
EVERY HOUR

I have dreamed a lot of dreams and seen many of them materialize. God, for reasons best known to Him, has been abundantly good to me. But after all these years of fast-paced busyness for Him and of conquering frontiers that loomed large in front of me, I find that beyond and under it all I still have a yearning in the core of my being that keeps drawing my attention toward God.

While I have given Him the best years and have maximized my energies for Him, I have found that busyness for Him has not drawn me closer to Him. In fact, in some ways it creates a false and treacherous sense of spirituality. It causes one to assume that spirituality is a performance; that intimacy with God is a business arrangement. It creates a flat and dull sort of Christianity that begins to turn our hearts cold and even sour if we are not careful.

I am awakening to the reality that we do ourselves no favor when we act and live as though Christianity were a stage on which we are to perform as though there were no deep need of an intimate relationship with the One who is the focus of our activity.

I have begun to sense as well that, in the abundance of God's goodness to me, I am prone to lose touch with the reality of how much I need Him. I know I need Him—my problem is that I find it easy to lose touch with the reality and ramifications of that knowledge. Early on in life and ministry, my sense of need was apparent in that we made less than our expenses, and without His gracious, over-and-above provision we would not have made it. We needed Him. My insecurities as a minister and public figure kept me very much aware of how much I needed Him. Each new church that we shepherded challenged my sense of self-sufficiency. Coming to Moody only compounded my sense of need.

At the same time, God, as He has with all of us, has given me gifts that enable me to be fruitful. These gifts and His wisdom make it possible to do relatively well at the challenges at hand. I'm a third-generation minister, so some of my capacity for ministry is instinctive. My income, by His gracious provision, is now more than adequate. I have served long enough at Moody to know the ropes and to enjoy what God has built me to do.

And now all of these gifts of His grace threaten my sense of need for Him. But I do need Him. Desperately. Now more than ever.

In all of this soul-searching about longing for Him and needing Him, I have been and continue to be deeply committed to Him. I believe that I would die for Him if necessary. I have had the unexpected privilege of being used by Him in ways that I never dreamed or expected. Yet this longing in my soul is real, and I am realizing that my tendencies toward independence and self-sufficiency are debilitating my ability to get closer to Him. If I don't believe I need Him, I probably won't desire Him.

When we forget that we need Him, our Christianity becomes little more than a task maintained by responsibilities and requirements. He really doesn't need to do much for us. We are pretty well set. While we count on Him for the big things—redemption, bailing us out if life goes in the ditch (only to find that since we have failed to develop intimacy with Him in the good times we don't know how to reach for Him in the bad times)—we have missed the pleasure and wonder of needing Him and being in touch with His presence and power that alone can satisfy, sustain, and secure us as an ongoing experience of life.

The history of African-Americans in our country is one marked with the necessity of needing God. As slaves they had little, life was hard, and there was no hope of gain or release. Yet their tradition is rich with a sense of reliance on God. It is evident in their music, like the spiritual that sings,

Oh, when I am alone, when I am alone,
Oh, when I am alone, give me Jesus.
Give me Jesus, give me Jesus.
You may have all this world, give me Jesus.

God looks for this kind of adoring devotion and dependency from us, but for the most part He gets little of either.

How can we who have so much of the abundant gifts of His gracious bounty, who have the constant presence of God in and around our lives live at such a distance? How can we feel so alone at the depth of our own souls? Well, I've had enough. I've had enough of a life that keeps stalling on the way home. I live with a renewed desire for greater intimacy with God.

As stark as that sounds, that is really how I feel. And while my life has not been technically without God in some ways, it has been a life that has yet to cultivate the kind of adoring dependency that is required to experience Him most fully and to be most powerfully used of Him.

It's not that I haven't felt His touch. I have. In some very special ways. In fact, those periodic brushes with His wonderful reality are part of what drives me to live in the constancy of His touch. And it's not that I haven't loved Him. I do. It's that I stand ready and wanting to know more of Him and to know Him in a more personal and intimate way. I want to go deeper with God. I am hearing the longing of my soul for more of Him.

15

Want to come along?

This pilgrimage takes us to the center of our own being. Not that the pursuit of God is a selfish thing. It's that the center of our being is where God meets us. Following the allure of this longing takes us to our own souls. It is an intensely personal and, ultimately, an intimately pleasurable pursuit.

Realistically, we will never know intimacy with Him in the fullest measure. That is the privilege reserved for us when we step to the other side and have the lens of our souls wiped finally and fully clean to see Him face-to-face. But until then, the healthiest and most fulfilling pursuit of life is to turn our lives toward that day and focus our lives on getting as good a look as possible now—to connect with Him as intimately as permissible.

I'm struck by the fact that Scripture begins with Adam and Eve in a safe, satisfying fellowship with God. Torn from Him by self-sufficiency, the rest of history is the story of humanity's attempt to live successfully apart from Him. Yet, the search to find satisfaction within ourselves and the careful erection of structures that supposedly sustain us apart from God consistently fail. Not one has succeeded.

Only He can fill the void. He is what we are looking for. And, in the end—which will be the eternal beginning—He will wipe away every tear and restore those who are His to that Eden-type of perfect fellowship forever, when we will triumphantly experience what John promises, "Behold, the tabernacle of God is among men, and He will dwell among them, and they shall be His people, and God Himself will be among them" (Revelation 21:3). And it is then that "happily-ever-after" will no longer be a dream or even a cynical laugh about the fairyland called eternal life. It will be a pulsating reality.

Until then, God beckons us to turn toward home—to begin the process of getting closer. To connect and enjoy Him and His resources more fully. He doesn't play cosmic games of hide-and-seek. He meets us where we are and helps us build momentum toward Himself. Life is best when it leans toward a deeper, more satisfying relationship with God. It is safest and most secure when we find our sustenance in all of life's situations in our connectedness to Him.

Regardless of who we are and what we have or do not have, the ultimate issue of life is where do I look for real satisfaction, and where can I be assured of sufficient resources to sustain and secure me regardless? If we don't seek to be satisfied and sustained in all the right places, we will be finally disappointed, left alone without hope, and in despair.

As I lay down this manuscript, I must admit that I feel a sense of frustration, knowing that there is so much more I would like to say and certainly more that needs to be written about moving from a sense of soulish isolation to a satisfying experience of intimacy with God.

Therefore, until someone picks up this topic from here, let this reflection be a primer, a starting point in the wonderful adventure of finding satisfaction, security, and sustenance in a growing intimacy with God. In a sense, this is a topic that will always beg for more, for we will never know intimacy in its fullest dimensions until we are truly home. But until then, it is our privilege to begin the process of turning from the aloneness of our own self-sufficiency to the fullness of a connected, God-sufficient experience.

Intimacy and aloneness stand at the opposite ends of our existence. Throughout Scripture and the experience of mankind, aloneness is the judgment on a life that chooses to be satisfied and sustained apart from God. Like the Prodigal Son, we need to pick ourselves up and turn our hearts toward home. The Father is graciously waiting. When He sees us coming, He runs to meet us. He must wonder why it has taken so long.

This chapter taken from Far From Home, *Moody Publishers, 1998*

T W O

✍

Crowding
Him Out

Martha breathes a quiet sigh of relief as she realizes both the kids are napping. That doesn't happen often these days now that the older one is four. It seems that her entire life revolves around the needs of two small children. Each day has become a continual cycle of feeding, cleaning up, washing, telling stories, and playing on the floor. These precious moments to herself are few and far between.

She can't help but wonder what her life would be like if she hadn't had kids. Her husband drives off to the office each morning and seems oblivious to what he's leaving behind for her to do. When he comes home and complains about all the problems and injustices of his work, she can't help but feel a bit jealous. Five years ago she had a job of her own and was well on her way to becoming partner in a small but growing advertising agency. She would probably be making more than Fred by now, but she had devoted herself to motherhood. She loves her husband and kids, yet she can't help but miss the challenges of business and the interaction she had with fellow workers—opportunities to really use her mind. She fears she will never have that opportunity again.

But even now, she knows that the money and stimulus of a challenging career would grow old and routine, leaving her looking for something that would really satisfy and sustain her soul.

Martha would tell you that what really haunts her is the memory of her former uncluttered growing walk with Christ—before He was crowded out. Not intentionally. Just incrementally—bit by bit, choice by choice, busyness by busyness. Back then she was onto something deeper—something more satisfying.

Mark is in his early thirties. He is from a large, active family that was always involved in team sports and a variety of social activities. People his age don't play team sports so much any more, and golf isn't his idea of exercise. He and his wife of five years have prepared for a large family of their own, but are having trouble getting pregnant. An emptiness nags him. No longer does he have the bustle of activity around him all the time. His house seems eerie and quiet, which makes him uncomfortable. He and his wife have talked so much about their situation that neither of them has much to say anymore.

His experience of church, Christianity, and other Christians has become routine and flat. They stay in the routines and rituals of their commitment to Christ but any sense of meaning and fulfillment is sporadic at best. Their lives for the most part are no different from the lives of those millions who have no connection to Christ.

He is beginning to lose hope that his life will ever be anything close to what he had planned. His wife, too, seems to be suffering from an inner depression she can hardly admit to herself, much less to him. But how can he help her when he doesn't know how to handle the submerged vacancy in his own soul?

I'm not much for jigsaw puzzles, but I know enough about them to know that you need all the pieces to enjoy a satisfying outcome. In many ways life is like a thousand-piece puzzle. We spend our days putting it together, hoping to create something meaningful out of all the scattered pieces. But when we can't find the strategic pieces that complete the picture, disappointment is unsettling at best and despair inducing at worst.

Honest philosophers have been telling us for centuries that, left to itself, life can be lonely, meaningless, and empty. Disappointment and despair are to be expected as normal by-products of our existence. The remedies proposed range from the passive resignation of a life stuck in the byword *whatever* to engagement in any experience that provides the adrenaline rush of temporary hits of excitement. Even the writer of Ecclesiastes searched the depths of wisdom, pleasure, wealth, and work to find meaning and satisfaction, but came up disillusioned. His conclusion is painfully honest.

> Then I became great and increased more than all who preceded me in Jerusalem. My wisdom also stood by me. All that my eyes desired I did not refuse them. I did not withhold my heart from any pleasure, for my heart was pleased because of all my labor and this was my reward for all my labor. Thus I considered all my activities which my hands had done and the labor which I had exerted, and behold all was vanity and striving after wind and there was no profit under the sun. *Ecclesiastes 2:9–11*

As one observer notes, "Life is like a wild goose chase without the goose."

In our most honest moments, we have all wondered why life is not more rewarding. Even our best experiences rarely leave much of lasting value, and often the anticipation is more fulfilling than the experience itself. We "channel surf" life, looking—hoping—for something to catch our attention, only to end up bored, jaded, and flat. And, when life gets in our face, we are shocked at how brutal and unconsoling it can be. In our quiet moments, we feel stalked by a sense of emptiness and fear.

We wonder, *Why? What is missing?*

Has anyone noticed that the one thing the philosophers, the meaning searcher in Ecclesiastes, and many of us have in common is that God has been removed as the preeminent center of our existence? When God is banished from human experience or relegated to the religious margins of our lives, left only to serve us on an "on call" basis, we become functionally alone. And when that happens, emptiness and vulnerability become more than philosophical theory. They are naked reality.

Are followers of Christ exempt?

No.

Even those of us who are connected to God through redemption often live our lives as though He isn't particularly relevant to the everyday occasions and encounters of life. We are proficient at maintaining the level of religious activity we deem appropriate, but God is hardly the throbbing center of our lives.

Yet He is supposed to be. And until He is, life is always less—far less—than it could be. Sometimes tragically less.

Unfortunately, we get used to life at a distance from God and become resigned to its not being what it is cracked up to be. We end up thinking that a close, satisfying relationship with God is only what others experience. And, even though He has offered us nearness, God seems inaccessibly far away.

And so we give up. Like amputee war veterans, we know how much we miss what we've lost, but, having no hope of getting it back, we adjust.

But life at a distance always has its downside. Not being in touch with God makes it difficult to depend and rely on Him. Living at a distance makes it easier to sin and to live in our sin—which only extends the distance. A creeping, quiet cynicism numbs our souls. When we hear the refrain, "Draw near to God and He will draw near to you" (James 4:8), we relegate it to the category of biblical statements we must believe but will probably never experience.

Yet the statement is true!

Those who draw near to God do find Him drawing near to them. God is the rewarder of those who "diligently seek Him" (Hebrews 11:6 KJV). There are legions who could testify to the pleasure of the experience.

The fault is not God's. We are not victims of some cosmic scam.

⁓

The fault is told in the parable of the Prodigal Son, found in Luke 15:11–32, perhaps Jesus' best-known and most-retold story. It is reflective of our experience with God, for in some measure the Prodigal's story is ours too.

The parable begins: "A man had two sons. The younger of them said to his father, 'Father, give me the share of the estate that falls to me.' So he divided his wealth between them" (Luke 15:11–12).

We aren't told why the younger son made this request. It wasn't even protocol for him to do so. Perhaps he felt like the low man on the totem pole in his household. Maybe he had a passion to make a name for himself. Maybe the older brother was hassling him. Maybe he was just bored. But it is safe to speculate that, in addition to any other reasons he may have had for leaving, chief among them was that he didn't know what a good thing he had. He lived in comfort and safety with a loving father, but this seemed tame compared to the allure of the world outside.

So he chose to leave.

And his father, for whatever reason, granted the request. He gave his son his portion of the inheritance and the freedom to walk away—and watched as he took to the road, intent on reaching a far country where he could live a more exciting life.

God is like that father, and often we are prone to be like that son. When we say that God is far away, it is we who have left, not He. Perhaps we have consciously or unconsciously held God at arms' length. We have wanted Him, but not wanted Him to interfere. Or we have feared that He would demand too much and that, having Him, we would have nothing else. Or our lives are so full of His abundant bounty that we have come to believe that we are not truly alone without Him—that we have all we need; that we really don't need Him. Or we may not have known how to draw near. Or the pace and crush of life has kept us from pursuing what we do know about intimacy with God.

Whatever the reason, our lives are the poorer for it. In fact, our lives are at risk because of it. The further we are from God, the further we are from the three essential ingredients we really need—really want—out of life. It is He who wants, and He alone who is able, to satisfy, sustain, and secure us. Without Him we are too frail to ward off the forces of life that are beyond our control. We are too compulsive, shortsighted, and misguided to find in-depth satisfaction and sustenance on our own. And when He is at a distance, we are easy targets for Satan's seductive allures. Sin and its debilitating consequences lie in ambush for those who stray far from God.

We are the prodigals. It is we who have left home. We are the ones who have been seduced and consumed by lesser allures. We, not God, are in the far country, and when we come to know how wonderful He is and how alone and empty we are, our hearts will long for home.

Tracking toward intimacy with God is not merely a nice thing to do. It is a necessary pursuit if we are to be safe in life and fulfilled at the core of our being. To experience life as He meant it to be, to be fulfilled as He intends us to be and sustained and secure as He wishes us to be, means that we begin the rewarding adventure of closing the gap.

Wanting Him and Him alone to fill our empty hearts, we pick up what is left of ourselves and head for home. At first we find it difficult to see clearly down the road, but with the help of other pilgrims we soon catch our pace, and the nearer we draw the more familiar the landmarks become. There's the church that we attend, and as we pass we see the days gone by when our hearts filled with joy as we sang His praises and served His people. There's the park bench where we used to sit and feel His closeness as we contemplated the beauty and wonder of His creation. And our Bible. And that special room where we spent precious times of fellowship with God in prayer. And our friends, who used to hold us accountable. We can still remember those times of prayer on Saturday mornings with them . . .

Who is that running to meet us?

Could it be God? We've been away so long and our choice to live in the far country has been such a sadness . . . such an offense to Him.

What we have not known is that His face has been turned toward the horizon watching, waiting to see if today might be the day we would come home. He's been there all the time.

It is He. His compassion embraces us. We are stunned by His grace and fall in humble repentance at His feet. He lifts us up and turns us toward home. He calls for the robe . . . for the ring and sandals. He begins the celebration and demands the fatted calf.

For the first time in a long time, we feel how good it is to be home where we belong. Chasing the aloneness into the shadows begins by seeking our satisfaction and sustenance at home —where God is.

While we have life and breath, God will not cease to pursue a rewarding, deepening intimacy with us. He is not content to leave us alone. His unceasing, unconditional love for each of us compels Him. He wants to meet us at the intersection of every dream, every desire, every choice, every thought, and He urges us to turn toward Him and actualize the finished work of His Son, the gift of the Spirit, and the resource of His Word. He welcomes us to begin a pilgrimage that puts our backs toward the aloneness in our souls and turns our faces toward the spectacular glow of intimacy with Him—toward life the way it was meant to be.

This chapter taken from Far From Home, *Moody Publishers, 1998*

I n a quiet subdivision in Lake in the Hills, Illinois, a rare blue heron stumbled into a steel trap designed to catch invading muskrats. Nancy Monica, a nearby neighbor, came to the heron's rescue, holding the bird still while a rescue worker freed its broken leg from the jaws of the trap.

What Nancy did not realize was that herons are very unpredictable in nature and, when cornered, will attack whatever is nearest. The injured bird began to peck at its rescuers with its razor-sharp beak. Thanks to the efforts of Nancy and the rescue worker, the bird was free to recover from its injured leg. Nancy Monica, however, sported a black eye.

Like that frightened bird, we sometimes do not recognize the One who has come to set us free. Scripture teaches us that God is busy seeking to relieve us from the entanglements of sin. He uses the reproofs of life and the consequences of sin to catch our attention. Like a loving father, He disciplines us to turn our hearts back to Him and His ways. To the church at Laodicea, Jesus said, "Those whom I love, I reprove and discipline; therefore be zealous and repent" (Revelation 3:19). Yet we tend to resist the reproofs and despise the discipline. It is easier to blame others for the consequences of our sin than it is to admit that God is trying to reach us and free us from our faults. It's not until we submit to the reproofs and surrender to the discipline that we will begin the process of yielded repentance that leads to freedom and purity.

Don't think that His gracious pursuit of you will go away. He is determined to finish the work that He began in our lives (Philippians 1:6). He was battered and bruised by our sin at the cross, and if He didn't give up there He is not going to now. He wants to feel us ceasing to struggle and to repentantly yield to His loving work.

This chapter taken from Strength for the Journey, *Moody Publishers, 2002*

The meal was just about finished when I leaned over and asked Billy Graham the question I had hoped to ask him all evening.

Martie and I had been seated next to Dr. Graham at a dinner for the staff and board of his organization. Billy, eighty at the time, was lucid and interesting. Wondering what he would say about his highest joys in life, I asked, "Of all your experiences in ministry, what have you enjoyed most?"

Then (thinking I might help him out a little), I quickly added, "Was it your time spent with presidents and heads of state? Or was it—"

Before I could finish my next sentence, Billy swept his hand across the tablecloth, as if to push my suggestions onto the floor.

"None of that," he said. "By far the greatest joy of my life has been my fellowship with Jesus. Hearing Him speak to me, having Him guide me, sensing His presence with me and His power through me. This has been the highest pleasure of my life!"

It was spontaneous, unscripted, and clearly unrehearsed. There wasn't even a pause.

With a life full of stellar experiences and worldwide fame behind him, it was simply Jesus who was on his mind and on his heart. His lifelong experience with Jesus had made its mark, and Billy was satisfied.

I found Billy Graham's statement that evening more than convicting. I found it motivating—right to the core of my being. With everything in me, I want what he's experienced. I found my heart saying, *If I make it to eighty, I want to say the same thing.*

Even more so when you consider the story of Chuck Templeton.

Templeton's name was practically a household word in evangelical homes in the fifties and sixties. He pastored one of Toronto's leading churches and—along with his close friend Billy Graham—helped found Youth for Christ in Canada. His extraordinary ability to communicate God's Word put him in demand on platforms all over North America.

But I don't remember him for his stellar gifts. I remember him for his renunciation of the faith. Evangelicals everywhere were rocked by the news that Chuck Templeton had left his church and renounced all he had previously embraced and proclaimed. The former preacher went on to fame and fortune. He managed two of Canada's leading newspapers, worked his way into an influential position with the Canadian Broadcasting Company—even took a run at the prime minister's office.

It had been decades since I'd thought of Chuck Templeton. So imagine my surprise when I noticed he had been interviewed by Lee Strobel in his book *The Case for Faith.* After reading Templeton's most recent book, *Farewell to God: My Reasons for Rejecting the Christian Faith,* Strobel caught a plane to Toronto to meet with him. Though eighty-three and in declining health, the former preacher vigorously defended his agnostic rejection of a God who claimed to be love, yet allowed suffering across the world to go unchecked.

Then, toward the end of their time together, Strobel asked Templeton point-blank how he felt about Jesus. Instantly, the old man softened. He spoke in adoring terms about Jesus, concluding, "In my view He is the most important human being who has ever existed." Then as his voice began to crack, he haltingly said, "I . . . miss . . . Him!" What that, Strobel writes, tears flooded Templeton's eyes, and his shoulders bobbed as he wept.

Think of it. Billy Graham and Chuck Templeton, two friends who chose radically different paths through life. And near the end of their journeys, one has found Jesus to be his most prized possession, while the other weeps for having left Him long ago.

Cynics might say that you'd expect someone like Graham to have a close walk with Jesus—and that common, ordinary folk like the rest of us can't expect to get there. But my grandmother had it as well. And she was no Billy Graham.

Born of pioneer stock in Michigan, she married a frontier farmer and gave birth to her children in a drafty, second-floor corner bedroom at home. She simply kept house for her family, far away from the hustle and bustle of high society. No one but friends and family even knew her name. Yet she had tapped the secret as well.

And so can you. Stepping into a deepening experience with Jesus is something more than keeping short accounts with sin in our lives. It's beyond that. It is about getting far enough beyond self that we can see Him more clearly and desire Him more completely.

Let me explain. First, so there is no confusion, keeping clear ledgers in our lives is basic to experiencing Christ. As long as there is residual sin in our hearts there will always be a distance. In His Sermon on the Mount, Jesus said, "Blessed are the pure in heart, for they shall see God" (Matthew 5:8). And the tenses in that pronouncement are not future but present. In other words, if you are not pure in heart today, don't count on experiencing Christ in a compelling way.

It's really not complicated. If there is bitterness, unresolved anger, sensual thoughts and actions, pride, untruthfulness, or slander and gossip in your vocabulary, you're going to feel the distance. Jesus doesn't meet us on those playing fields. He'll meet us there to pull us out of the ditch of our own ways, but He won't stay there with us.

I hope you are in a quiet place where you can put this book down for a moment and think carefully about those things in your life that stand between you and Jesus. Go to your knees and open your life to His divine inspection. Pray as the psalmist prayed,

> Search me, O God, and know my heart;
> Try me and know my anxious thoughts;
> And see if there be any hurtful way in me,
> And lead me in the everlasting way. *Psalm 139:23–24*

Don't shy away from this. He already knows about your secret thoughts and struggles. He has been grieving the distance between your heart and His. At this very instant, He is waiting for you, His cleansing mercy readily available.

Excerpted from Simply Jesus, © *2002 by Dr. Joseph M. Stowell. Used by permission of Multnomah Publishers, Inc.*

F I V E

☙

Great
Expectations:
Getting Past
the Myths
About Intimacy

W hat does God tell us that we can truly expect as we search for intimacy with Him?

Expectations are everything. If we expect our spouse to be home at a certain time for dinner, and they aren't, if we expect our teenage son to come home early enough so that we can use the car to make our tee time, and he doesn't . . . it's a problem. When we expect friendship to be pleasant, rewarding, and uncomplicated, and it isn't; when we expect to receive that raise, that bonus, that promotion, and we don't, we inevitably feel disappointment, then discouragement, and finally despair if the broken expectation is big enough.

But finding satisfaction, sustenance, and security in our relationship with God is a process. Too many of us have become discouraged in the pursuit of God by expecting that the product will be ours quickly and that the experience will be in line with our expectations of what it ought to be.

What can we realistically expect? As we have learned, the first task in the pursuit of intimacy is to deal with the disconnectedness that keeps us far from home. This is our responsibility. God looks for repentant, radically reliant hearts in which to set up His residence.

Having dealt with life in the far country, the next step is starting on a pilgrimage toward God by being routinely faithful to the realities that trigger an experience with His fulfilling presence. When we are faithful about the process of connecting to God, He is consistently faithful about fulfilling us in His time and in His way. Each of us will experience Him differently. And He will respond to us differently at different seasons and intervals of life. The consistency and constancy of His reality in our lives will be a lifelong growth experience.

Intimacy with God must not be defined in terms of its experiential elements. Experiences are too subjective, varied, and individualized to nail down as universal scenarios of intimacy. God doesn't meet all of us in the same way, emotionally, intellectually, or spiritually. Each of us perceives things in a unique way. When we read biographies of Christians or hear someone tell of a close encounter he has had with God, we shouldn't try to frame our own experiences to match. God meets us where *we* are and not where someone else is.

While none of us experiences God in precisely the same way, all of us do come home by way of the same road map. We do the process; God responds with an individualized product. In fact, this is what Scripture teaches us when we are told to "draw near to God and He will draw near to you" (James 4:8). That is a process statement.

I remember talking with a quality-control expert about his job as a consultant to some of the leading industries in America. I had always thought that quality control was about standing at the end of the line, looking products over, and, if they were not made well, sending them back to be rebuilt. Wrong! He told me that the key to quality control was to create a process that was effective and efficient. If the process was right, the product was guaranteed. It was the process that guaranteed the product.

What is the operational definition of the process that keeps our soul turned toward home? The pursuit of intimacy is an intentional commitment to take steps toward God and, in the process of that Godward motion, to grow more deeply conscious of, connected to, and confident in Him alone as the only source to satisfy, sustain, and secure. The pursuit is a nonnegotiable commitment on my part to actively apply the principles that God has given us and to patiently and persistently build my life around them. They are the principles of

- a repentant turnaround in attitude and action;
- a repudiation of self-sufficiency that leads to a radical reliance on Christ;
- a conscious connecting in ongoing communication; and
- a connecting with Him in creation, in His character and conduct, in worship and praise, in crisis, and in faithful obedience.

A commitment to these principles empowers my consciousness of Christ, my connectedness to Christ, and my confidence in Christ. The pursuit of intimacy with God embraces a way of life that increasingly fills my soul with the satisfaction, sustenance, and security of His presence. The pursuit of intimacy is about growing more deeply connected to Christ as the ultimate source for all that I need.

While it's important to have a definition of the pursuit of intimacy as our starting point, we should be careful to see that the process is not sabotaged by myths that distort our perspective. Part of defining deals with clarifying what is not true as well as embracing what is true.

Myth #1: Intimacy is primarily about what He will do for us when we get close.

The process of intimacy should never be motivated by what God might do for us but rather by our desire to do what we can for Him.

In 1985 the race to win the then-Eastern Division of the American League came down to one game at the end of the season. Frank Tanana was on the mound for the Detroit Tigers and pitched a brilliant game to bring his team to victory, 2–1. I still remember seeing the picture of Frank, arms lifted in ecstatic celebration, on the cover of the next day's *USA Today,* and reading all the praise of the press for what a great pitcher he was.

Several days later Frank pitched in the American League championship series. If the Tigers could clinch this championship, they would advance to the World Series. But Frank didn't do as well this time. In fact, the Tigers lost the game and ultimately the series. This time the talk was all about Frank's less-than-spectacular performance.

I was Frank's pastor, and a few days after the game I asked him, "How do you deal with being a hero one minute and the bad guy the next?" He said to me, "Joe, I learned something a long time ago about baseball fans. The deal with baseball fans is, they all live by 'What have you done for me today?' That's all that counts."

Later, I reflected on his comments and realized that that attitude characterizes a lot of us as God's people. When we think about intimacy, it's easy to envision it in terms of "What has God done for me today?" And if the answer to that is "Nothing," we might find ourselves asking, "What has God done for me lately?" We tend to validate His reality and measure the quality of our relationship to Him by what He is doing for us at any given moment and by the frequency and intensity of His interventions in our lives. Is there any one of us who hasn't assumed that the reality of God and the quality of our relationship to Him is measured by how many times He drops into our lives and does something good and spectacular?

When this is our expectation, we quickly grow disinterested, discouraged, even dysfunctional in our walk with Him. In my own life I've often felt cheated. If I hear someone talk about the marvelous intervention of God in his life and the spectacular things God has done, I begin to wonder why God never does anything like that for me.

Do you ever feel spiritually abnormal because God just doesn't seem to be doing a lot for you? Have you ever felt a lack of spiritual self-esteem, as though maybe you're not all that important to God? Or have you ever felt as though

He might well be the God of our fathers but was surely out of the office in our generation? It's kind of like Lewis Carroll's *Alice in Wonderland,* where the complaint is lodged: "Jam tomorrow, and jam yesterday, but never jam today."

I think that's why a lot of us are seduced by anything that is spiritually experiential. If the recipe comes in the guise of Christianity, even if it's wildly exotic, we flock to it so that we can sense that God is doing something "real" for us. Rather than continuing to faithfully take the routine steps toward God in our pilgrimage, we wait by the side of the road looking for a holy handout. It's always easier to opt for the quick hit, the rush of spiritual adrenaline, than to focus on the long haul.

Rangers in Yellowstone Park tell us that, in spite of all the signs that say "Don't feed the bears," people are constantly doing just that. As a result, rangers have to pick up dead bears in the woods who died from starvation because tourists weren't there to feed them. If there are no handouts for two weeks, the bears die. And to think that the woods are full of nourishment! The bears could have gotten busy about what they were built to do, but instead they died because they tried to get by on the easy handouts.

We are like those bears. God has provided an abundance of nourishment for us to feed on if we are tracking toward Him through prayer, Bible reading, fellowship with other Christians, and practicing the commands of Scripture. If we are faithful, none of us is going to starve. In fact, our spiritual hunger should drive us to seek out more of the good things of God. He calls us to be fed and nourished by Him at the core of our beings, yet we keep looking for easy, quick hits of His presence. It makes me wonder if heaven contains signs that say, "Don't feed the Christians!" Intimacy is not about holy handouts. It is characterized by steadfast faithfulness.

We can see this truth throughout the life of Abraham. God motivated him to leave Ur of the Chaldees with a whole list of promises (Genesis 12). Abraham obeyed God even though he had not yet received the promised son. When Sarah got too old to have a baby, she and Abraham were very confused about

God's will. They even tried to fulfill His will through their own maneuverings. Yet Abraham continued to worship God and track toward intimacy with Him. God kept His promise, and Isaac was born. Later, when God told Abraham to sacrifice Isaac, Abraham was faithful to the command and was willing to obey. God again kept His promise by sparing Isaac's life. Abraham committed himself to the process of obedience, and God intervened time after time with a new and deeper level of intimacy.

It's easy to think we would all be faithful if God intervened in our lives the way He did with Abraham, but we forget that the story of Abraham covers decades. The recorded interventions of God into Abraham's life average about one every fifteen years. Think about going fifteen years without having a Bible, with no indwelling Spirit, without spiritual friends, and not hearing from God. Yet he lived a life of steadfast faithfulness to God.

When Joseph was seventeen, God gave him a dream that someday he would stand in great authority and even his brothers would bow to him. But that's the last dream he had from God for many years. In the meantime, his jealous brothers ganged up on him and sold him as a slave. His owner's wife tried day after day to seduce him and eventually falsely accused him of attempted rape. He was sent to jail, where he helped out a guy who promised to repay the favor but forgot about him. Yet Joseph stayed faithful to God.

God could have appeared at any time and bailed Joseph out of a problem situation, but He didn't. Instead, He worked behind the scenes silently arranging the time when Joseph would emerge humbled and refined. Joseph was ready to be wonderfully used by God, and God delivered him. Joseph's simple, steadfast faithfulness led to power in his life (Genesis 41:39–45).

Job was clueless as to what God was doing in his life. I find it interesting that God never explained that the devil was actually behind Job's sufferings (Job 1:1–2:6). But after Job exemplified steadfast faithfulness, God intimately revealed Himself and helped Job resolve the conflict of his soul (38:1– 40:2; 40:6–41:34).

The willingness to serve faithfully while waiting to receive God's promises is not limited to Old Testament characters. Paul knew what it meant to remain steadfast in the midst of difficult circumstances. He wrote: "We are afflicted in every way, but not crushed; perplexed, but not despairing; persecuted, but not forsaken; struck down, but not destroyed; always carrying about in the body the dying of Jesus, so that the life of Jesus also may be manifested in our body" (2 Corinthians 4:8–10). In the same context, he adds: "We look not at the things which are seen, but at the things which are not seen; for the things which are seen are temporal, but the things which are not seen are eternal" (v. 18). In essence, Paul was saying that our lives should be driven by the reality of eternity to come, not by here-and-now experiences.

We may think that Christianity is about God pleasing us, but Paul makes it clear that our ambition in life should be to please Him. That is the essence of authentic Christianity. God rarely invades our lives with dramatic interventions. And when He does, it is not only for our benefit but to reveal His glory through us (1 Chronicles 16:9–10). While it's true that God loves to be generous with us and gives us many good things, we have to realize that when it comes to the major interventions, He manages the agenda.

Romance requires our steadfast faithfulness—as well as our charm, personality, money, and everything else—to finally win the day. But as you learn to put the other person first, you discover the joy of what love is all about. You won't know the thrill of an intimate relationship until you faithfully pursue the other person.

So it is with our relationship to God. In the pursuit of God, we are responsible for routine faithfulness. Eventually the reward will come. Intimacy is about faithfulness now and fulfillment then . . . in God's time.

Myth #2: Intimacy is about an informal buddy-buddy relationship with God.

There's no doubt that an important element of our relationship with God is built on the fact that His Word welcomes us to call Him "Abba! Father!"

(Galatians 4:6). When we are close to someone, we are usually on a first-name basis. Christ tells us that we are no longer slaves but friends (John 15:15). Yet there is far more to an ongoing relationship with God than backslapping chumminess. Intimacy with God is about being struck with His grandeur and majesty. We need to stand with reverent hearts in awe at the thought of a relationship with Him.

Think of it this way. If Christ were to walk into the room while you were reading this chapter, what would you do? When Martie gets lost in a book, my only hope is to say, "When you come out of book-world, I have a question I want to ask you," which usually elicits a distant, audible noise that registers as an acknowledgment of my request.

But none of us would be lost in book-world if Christ walked into the room.

Some of us might think we would get out that list of questions we always wanted to ask Him. Others of us imagine jumping up and throwing our arms around Him and thanking Him for saving us. Perhaps the more exuberant types envision giving Him a high five for all He is and all He has done.

I can assure you that if Christ walked into the room while you were reading this book, none of the above would occur. We would fall flat on our faces before Him, feeling phenomenally undone, exposed, unworthy. Thankfully, He would come near, lift us up, and tell us not to be afraid. By His grace, He would welcome us into His presence that we might know the joy of His fellowship. But our relationship with Him would always be marked by a sense of awe and respect, even when we enjoyed sweet moments of close fellowship with Him.

Myth #3: The experience of intimacy is the same for all of us.

The expectation of a universal standard of intimacy with God usually falls somewhere between highly charged emotional experiences and deep, quiet personal encounters at the depth of the soul. While both are valid ways in which we can experience intimacy with God, it is dangerous to try to pour ourselves into the mold of someone else's experience.

I've always been intrigued by the temperament and personality differences among the disciples. The breadth and mix of their differences guaranteed that none of them experienced intimacy with Christ in the same way or at the same level. There was Thomas, who was highly cognitive, wanting to analyze and reason everything through to his full satisfaction. There was Peter, who was quick, verbal, and aggressive. And there was John, who was soft, warm, and mellow. Some of us will experience intimacy with Christ as a cognitive and intellectual experience, as it probably was for Thomas. Others of us will experience intimacy in the emotional side of our beings. People from different cultures and different backgrounds and with different personalities will experience Christ in a wonderful variety of ways.

What we will have in common, as we have already learned, will not be the *nature* of our experience of intimacy with Christ but the *process* through which we move toward that intimacy. If we are to encourage one another toward deeper, more meaningful experiences with God, we should not flaunt or promote our own experiences as the standard, but rather help one another stay in the process.

Myth #4: We can experience the fullness of intimacy with God in the here and now.

It is vitally important to remember that God's Word tells us that now "we see through a glass, darkly; but then face to face" (1 Corinthians 13:12 KJV)! We will never know the fullness of the joy of unhindered intimacy with God on this side of heaven. Our limitations are too severe.

We are encased in bodies and have minds that are still affected by the Fall. After Eden, sweat and fatigue became a way of life. The physical state of our bodies affects our minds and emotions. When we are drained of energy, we experience God's presence in far different ways than during times of strength and vitality. If I had the opportunity, I would spend large blocks of time sitting on a cliff overlooking the vast expanse of His creation, walking through the countryside, or letting my eyes plumb the depths of the starry universe above me. The problem is, those times are few and far between.

I try to carve out time in the mornings just to spend with God. But after a wonderful time of reading His Word, praying, and meditating on Him, I have to throw myself headlong into the busyness of my day. God is still there to help and encourage me, but my day and its routines and challenges cloud the specialness of those quiet moments at the beginning of my day.

Yet my work is part of my responsibility to serve Him. We all were put on Earth to do more than experience His presence in quiet corners. Now is not the stage in life to spend all our time in contemplative solitude. The world around us needs to hear about Him. Hurting people need help. Despairing neighbors need the encouragement that only God can provide through us. Our employers need a good day's work from us.

Not being able to sense deep intimacy with God all the time should motivate us to live for the day when we will see Him face-to-face. Soon enough, the baggage of our fallenness, the press of life's responsibilities, will be lifted from our backs and the cares of this life will evaporate. In the twinkling of an eye, we will find ourselves in an eternity where the prime preoccupation will be to enjoy unhindered intimacy with Him. Forever.

Myth #5: We can experience intimacy with a partially surrendered life.

The experience of true intimacy with God does not require perfection, but it does require that we be fully surrendered. Full surrender means that we live with an attitude of unlimited obedience. Though we may fail, refusing to become entrenched in our failure by an immediate response of repentance will keep us on the path toward home.

It would be hard to believe that we could have intimacy in an earthside relationship in the fullest, most rewarding sense if we were living in continuing offense toward the one with whom we were seeking to develop intimacy. Many marriages suffer a loss of intimacy because one of the partners has ceased to be loyal. Lying to or cheating on a spouse, ignoring the other's needs, using the relationship for your own benefit when it's convenient and neglecting responsibilities when it's convenient are all prescriptions for a quick distancing between two hearts.

So it is with God. All through Scripture God requires that we give Him the totality of our beings. We are to love the Lord our God with all our heart, strength, and mind (see Deuteronomy 6:5; Matthew 22:37; Mark 12:30). In the letters Christ wrote to the churches in the early chapters of the book of Revelation, it was their ongoing, undealt-with sin and shortcomings that shortchanged their relationship with Christ.

We cannot expect intimacy when we live like Wilbur Reese described when he said:

> *I'd like to buy three dollars' worth of God.*
> *Please, not enough to explode my soul or disturb my sleep, but*
> *just enough to equal a cup of warm milk or a snooze in the sunshine. I*
> *don't want enough of Him to make me love a black man or pick beets*
> *with a migrant.*
> *I want ecstasy, not transformation. I want the warmth of the womb,*
> *not a new birth. I want about a pound of the eternal in a paper sack.*
> *I'd like to buy about three dollars' worth of God, please.*

Pushing the myths aside clears the way for the process of our progress toward God to take hold. It opens a realistic door to knowing and experiencing Him at new and rewarding levels.

I think I have a major starch deficiency in my life because I'm passionately addicted to potatoes, rice, and pasta. I can't get enough of them. If Martie is away for an evening, when she returns she will invariably ask me what I had for supper while she was gone. I have to tell her I just boiled some pasta and put a little butter and salt and pepper on it. She just looks at me in amazement.

What is more amazing to me is that often, when I'm full of pasta, I still want more.

That longing is similar to the wonder and joy of growing toward intimacy —we can never get enough of Christ. It's a never-ending, increasingly rewarding process. To help encourage the process, here are five truths that can help us form realistic expectations about intimacy with God.

Truth #1: Our primary purpose in life is to embrace the transcendent God by faith and to worship Him in purity and service.

Intimacy is not about God doing things for me. It's not about Him making me feel good. It's me embracing the transcendent God of the universe and pledging to worship and serve Him no matter what happens. When the arrows of my passions and my worship point from me to Him, I've successfully reversed the direction of my expectations. And as I worship Him with the purity of my life and the service of my hands, I can say with Job, no matter what happens, "Though He slay me, I will hope in Him" (Job 13:15). Intimacy begins by giving ourselves away—giving ourselves to God, as the ultimate gift of our love.

Truth #2: God intervenes in dramatic ways only periodically and selectively for major purposes in His kingdom and the blessings of His people.

That ought to be enough for us. It should be sufficient to hear about or to see God's work in somebody else's life and say, "Isn't that just like my God? I love to see God busy!" Instead, we tend to feel sorry for ourselves and complain, "That never happens to me. Why isn't God busy about me?" We should learn to rest and rejoice in the fact that God does marvelous things in others' lives, and that if our need ever gets dramatic enough or our place in His plan ever gets strategic enough, He'll do something dramatic for us as well. Until then, we need to be forever grateful for His daily presence; His quiet work behind the scenes; His grace that is sufficient; His mercy that stays His judgment; and heaven.

Truth #3: God has already done more for me than I deserve.

If God never does anything more than redeem us—cancel hell and guarantee heaven—if He never does anything more than that, He has already done more than we deserve. That ought to be enough to launch me in praise and worship for the rest of my life.

Think about it. God has already dramatically intervened in a major way in our lives when He opened up the story of the Cross to us and by the power of His Spirit bid us come. When we embraced that rugged cross and felt the weight of our sin leave us and His cleansing blood washed us clean, it was enough— more than enough to keep our hearts lovingly grateful.

Truth #4: God is probably doing a lot of things for us that we do not even know about.

These may not be big, dramatic things, but God's Word teaches us that He stands like a sovereign sentinel at the gates of our lives, keeping out anything that is more than we can bear (1 Corinthians 10:13). He only lets in those things that He, by His power and with our cooperation, will turn to His glory and gain and to our good. Paul declares in Romans 8:28, "We know that God causes all things to work together for good to those who love God, to those who are called according to His purpose."

Why then do we put our head on the pillow at night and murmur, "Where were You today, God? You didn't answer my prayer. Nothing big happened. The day was flat and dull"? Instead, we should say with hearts full of gratitude, "Lord, thanks for being busy in my life today in stuff I don't even know about. You, by the power of Your angels, have protected me from the Enemy who sought to destroy me. And thanks for the assurance that, as the sovereign sentinel at the gate of my life, what You did let in today, You promised that by Your power You could turn to glory and gain and good."

We have to remember that God is a lot busier in our lives than we think. For us to go around thinking that He doesn't do much for us contradicts the reality of His marvelous grace that is in our lives twenty-four hours a day: guarding, keeping, excluding, insulating, protecting, and blessing.

Truth #5: When God thinks of intimacy, He thinks of a heart relationship with us.

We're like kids at Christmas, begging, "Give me the gift! Give me the gift!" and forgetting that it's out of love that the gifts were given to us by our parents. Of course, our parents love to give to us and to bless us with gifts, but what they really want is a love relationship with us. Intimacy is about a relationship, not a gift exchange. When we live expectantly, serve Him purely, slow down and spend seasons on our knees with His Word in prayer and meditation, He fills our souls with Himself.

God doesn't meet us at the mall. He seeks us in the inner sanctum of our hearts. If it's intimacy we want, we need to be more intrigued with the Giver than the gifts. It's not the stuff He does for us that we should be loving; it's Him. If we want to experience Him more than we do, we need to love Him more than we do—more than all those other things we are attracted to, more than all the provisions we expect from Him.

This chapter taken from Far From Home, *Moody Publishers, 1998*

E rnest Hemingway, the literary genius, said this about his life: "I live in
a vacuum that is as lonely as a radio tube when the batteries are dead, and
there is no current to plug into."

This is a startling statement, given the fact that Hemingway lived his life
in a way that would be the envy of any person who had bought the values of our
modern society. Hemingway was known for his tough-guy image and globe-
trotting pilgrimages to exotic and faraway places. He was a big-game hunter,
a bullfighter, a man who could drink the best of them under the table. He was
married four times and lived his life seemingly without moral restraint or conscience. But on a sunny Sunday morning in Idaho, he pulverized his head with
a shotgun blast.

Not only does Hemingway stand as a symbol of the bankruptcy of a self-
managed life, but he also models for us another reality that very few people know
about. Ernest Hemingway grew up in a solid evangelical Christian home in Oak
Park, Illinois. His grandparents were missionaries, and his physician-father

was a devoted churchman and best of friends with evangelist Dwight Lyman Moody. Hemingway's family conformed to the strictest codes of Christianity, and as a boy and young man Hemingway was active in the life of his church, serving as a choirboy.

Then came the Great War, and Hemingway went away as a war correspondent and saw the death and despair that only a war on that scale can bring. His youthful enthusiasm for Christianity was soured to the point where he progressively, through the next several years, rejected his upbringing and denied the validity and credibility of the Christ that he once had embraced.

Or had he?

While we certainly don't know all that transpired, it would seem fair to say that Ernest Hemingway never developed a truly personal relationship with Christ. Living in an environment, going through catechism, conforming to the codes, and expressing a general affirmation of the truths of Scripture are not really what genuine Christianity consists of. Authentic Christianity is composed of non-negotiated followers who are progressively moving toward Christ and who understand all of life and all of this world in the context of His teaching and His truth. If we aren't cultivating a living, vital relationship with Jesus Christ, then we, too, can respond as Hemingway did when either life's questions are agonizingly unanswerable or when our inner impulses are too seductive for us to resist. Relating to systems, rituals, and rules as a point of allegiance is never enough to keep us unflinchingly loyal.

The point really is not Hemingway's life. It's my life and your life. The point is whether we are simply fellow travelers along for the ride for reasons other than Christ, or are genuinely pursuing a relationship with Him.

Scripture is crystal clear about the profile of a true follower of Jesus Christ. Interestingly, in the text in Matthew 4 that recounts the call of Christ to Andrew, Peter, James, and John, a different word is used for their response to Christ than the word that Christ used to call them. Christ's call means that we are to "come after Him." The essence of that call involves the direction of our lives.

But the word the disciples used to respond had an additional meaning. It was a technical word used of individuals in that day who were known by their friends and others around them as followers. According to linguistic scholars, it reflected two basic nuances. First, a follower was one who had a growing and deepening relationship to the one they were following. Followers do not think of their following as a task or project or duty. It is first and foremost a *relationship* to this person who is being followed.

Second, a true follower is in the process of a radical *reformation* because of the influence of the leader on her life. True followers do not remain the same once they start following Christ. He is involved in a task of radical reformation in our lives in terms of both character and conduct. Followers become imitators of the one they are following. You know a follower because he acts and reacts like the One who is leading his life.

So in the time of the disciples, someone who called you a "follower" of Christ would expect to see your life busy about relationship and reformation. This identity was so clear in Christ's day that calling someone a follower would be no different from saying of someone, "He's a trucker" or "She's a doctor." It defined the privilege and responsibility of their role as followers. It spoke volumes about who they were and explained why they lived, thought, and acted as they did.

The word for "follow" applied to Peter, Andrews, James, and John in Matthew 4:19-21 indicates a person who so longed to know the right way to live that he initiated a relationship with the local rabbi, knowing that the rabbi was the very epitome of God's truth about life as expressed in the Torah. The Torah contained God's revealed definitions and directives for life. It was God's means of managing instincts toward what was not only productive and good, but also toward what would bring glory to Him and gain to

His plans and purposes. Followers in the rabbinical sense were those who had so longed for God and His standards that they moved in with the local rabbi as a means of knowing and growing toward God. The closest you could get to God on earth was through the rabbi. So followers in the technical sense were those who attached themselves to the local rabbi. These individuals often left everything they owned to live with the rabbi. They would serve the rabbi, sit at his feet, watch him intently, and seek, by following him, to go where their longing to live God's way could be satisfied.

Christ is the "local rabbi" of our souls. He lures us with persistent love into a deepening relationship with Him. He is God, and a relationship with Him literally explodes with the love and leadership that we long for. He loves us all the way home to heaven. Following is, at the very heart of it all, a relationship with One who highly values intimacy with us and works to enable and empower it. I'm reminded of the words of St. Augustine: "Thou askest what thou shouldest offer for thee? Offer thyself. For what else doth the Lord seek of thee but thee?"[1]

I figure I have one more high-energy run in which to maximize my life for Him. And I find that in the deepest part of my being, I want this season to be marked by a followership that springs from a deepening intimacy with Christ.

If you like fishing, you know that casting a line toward the shore and pulling it back is essentially what it's all about. If the line is pulled back quickly, it covers a lot of territory but simply skims the surface. If you slow down as you retrieve it, it goes deeper and deeper — where, presumably, the fish wait.

I want to meet Him in those depths.

I suspect you do, too. But the question remains: How do I move into deepening intimacy with Him?

I believe there are (at least) six "principles of following" we can affirm:

- Christ wants to come into our lives through the door of our hearts. Followers take the initiative to welcome Him within.
- Christ stands ready to be found and known in prayer, His Word, and His active work in our lives and the world around us. Followers find Him in these privileged practices.
- Christ's presence is experienced when He is at the strategic center of all we are and do. Followers put Him there.
- Christ relates to us in the sphere of who He is, where He is, what He is, and what He wants to do. Followers meet Him in these places.
- Christ often leads us into and through crisis situations so that we become convinced of His reality and presence in our lives. Followers view crises as opportunities to experience Him more fully.
- Christ meets us, speaks to us, and touches us through the physical and visible reality of His body the church. Followers look for Him there.

We have all seen people who from a distance seem compelling. We would like to know them and develop a relationship with them. It was like that when I fell in love with my wife, Martie.

I can remember seeing Martie for the first time when she was a college freshman. I noticed her just a week or so after we had all arrived on campus, and each time I saw her there was something intriguing about her, even though it was seen from a distance. Soon I got the courage to ask her for her company for an evening, and she agreed. The more I got to know her, the more compelling a person she became. And it wasn't long until I was wanting a full-time, lifelong relationship with her. And when the big question was asked, she said yes. She is, after all these decades, still the most compelling person in my life.

I do not continue to live with Martie only because of vows or commitments I have made. Although they are vitally important and would keep me in the relationship if they were all that was left, I'm not in this for the "institution" of marriage. I don't continue to live with Martie just because it's the respectable thing to do, and people will think better of me if I am a loyal person. I am driven to be with her by the fact that she and I have a growing relationship with each other. It is the pleasure and the power of that relationship that affects not only my conduct toward her, but also the way I live all of my life. It's not that I'm perfect. She could tell you I am not! The bottom line of my attitudes and activities is the fact that I have a highly valued relationship with her.

That is exactly what it is like to be a follower of Christ. It's not the codes or the catechisms. It's Christ. Because I am His and He is mine, I gladly follow, sit at His feet, surrender, and serve.

Taken from Following Christ. *Hardcover by Joseph M. Stowell. Copyright © 1996 by Joseph M. Stowell. Used by permission of The Zondervan Corporation.*

TWO

HE TOUCHED ME

F rom her youth, Ruth Jordan McBride understood the harsher side of life.

Ruth's father, a Polish immigrant, eked out a living as an itinerant orthodox rabbi in Virginia. Her mother, a shy invalid who spoke broken English, endured frequent beatings from her violent husband. Eventually, Ruth's father gave up on his "calling" and bought a store. Ruth worked long hours and endured stinging verbal attacks and even sexual assaults by her father.

Tragically, Ruth spent most of her adolescent years looking for love. That search led her down dark and dangerous paths. It ultimately led her straight into the arms of a fella next door—a young black man who had become a regular customer. For the first time in her life she felt cared for. However, this discovery of love proved unsafe. Pregnant and shamed, she felt the scorn of her mother, who quietly sent her away to live in New York with a relative. There the pregnancy would be secretly "dealt with." When she returned home, Ruth made a painful discovery. Life would never again be the same. She went back to New York, where she met Rocky, who also promised love and protection. But he too offered the wrong sort of love—a love that led her into darker places than she had been before. Rocky was a pimp.

Again she fled. Broken, discouraged, and at the end of her rope, the young girl from Virginia had grown strangely old—with a hardness to her that ran deep in her soul. Then she met Dennis McBride—an unusually gentle man who loved her from the start. This time the love was real. She at once felt valued and dignified. She finally belonged.

Still, this love from a man was not enough to deliver her from years of pain and abuse.

Years later, Ruth told her son James the secret—the secret that enabled her to rise like a phoenix out of the ashes of her dad's abuse, a story he writes in the best-selling book *The Color of Water*.

In the book he describes how his mother reflected on the slurs she endured for marrying a black man. She said, "Well, I don't care. Your father changed my life. He taught me about God, who lifted me up and forgave me and made me new. I was lucky to meet him, or I would've been a prostitute or dead. Who knows what would've happened to me? I was reborn in Christ. Had to be, after all I went through."[1]

"Ma was utterly confused about all but one thing: Jesus . . . Jesus gave Mommy hope. Jesus was Mommy's salvation. Jesus pressed her forward. Each and every Sunday, no matter how tired, depressed or broke, she got up early, dressed in her best, and headed for church."[2]

He continues, "Even as a boy I knew God was all powerful because of Mommy's utter deference to him, and also because she would occasionally do something in church that I never saw her do at home or anywhere else: at some point in the service, usually when the congregation was singing one of her favorite songs like, 'We've Come This Far by Faith' or 'What a Friend We Have in Jesus,' she would bow down her head and weep. It was the only time I saw her cry. 'Why do you cry in church?' I asked her one afternoon after the service. 'Because God makes me happy. . . . I'm crying 'cause I'm happy.'"[3]

How do the Ruths of this world rise above the debilitating effects of brokenness, abuse, deep emotional burdens, bondage, and temptation, to hold their hands high in victory? Or for that matter, how do any of us escape the stranglehold of a world that, whether in good times or bad, obscures our capacity to live out our love for Jesus?

The answer is clear—and the answer holds our only hope. When those of us who are trapped in the brokenness of life or lost in the comfortable veneer of self-righteous religion come to grips with the true Lover of our souls, we experience radical change. A change that can only be driven by a love for Christ so compelling that it defines all we do—a love defined by the life-changing goodness that only He can bring. When we allow Christ to move us beyond mere mental assent into a vibrant relationship, we are compelled to express our love for Him in radical ways.

That's what happened to Ruth, and that's what happened to the sinning woman described in Luke 7. They both met Jesus, and their lives were never the same.

∽

Ruth McBride's transforming love for Christ is a carbon copy of the experience of the woman that we meet in Luke 7. We are introduced to this woman by the gospel writer who in thirteen verses describes what might be Scripture's most moving and instructive picture of what it means to love Christ. We are never told her name, but we are told that she was a woman "who had lived a sinful life" (Luke 7:37 NIV). Luke doesn't say exactly what gave her such a bad reputation, but the word he uses to describe her—sinner—is most often used in the Bible to refer to people whose lives were characterized by immorality. She was probably the town prostitute or, at best, a woman known for her loose morals. In ancient Jewish culture, being known as a "sinner" marked people like her as social outcasts. They were the lowest and most despised people in the community.

But her mention in the passage is not the most striking feature of Luke's narrative. We often read in the Gospels of sinners flocking to Jesus. But this woman showed up at Simon the Pharisee's home. Simon had a reputation of his own. He clearly stood out as the best, most religious person in town. A model of piety and godliness. Luke couldn't resist telling the story of how these two starkly different characters wound up in the same room with Jesus.

Luke intends that this sinner-saint encounter mark for us the huge distance between what motivated the sinful woman to act in love and what kept the pious Simon so incapable of truly loving Christ. Luke probes the essence of why it's hard to love Jesus. But this is far more than mere history. This story forces us to consider our own relationship to Him. Of course, we'd want to see ourselves at the Master's feet worshiping alongside the woman. But in all honesty, we may look more like Simon, enjoying the benefits of His presence, while keeping Him at arm's length!

Now, if you're feeling a bit uncomfortable, don't resist that feeling. It means that we're off to a good start. Sensing your need to change can mark the beginning of genuine transformation.

As the drama unfolds, we can't help but be amazed at the stunning quality of the woman's love. Courageous, bold, and quick to express itself regardless of risk.

Hearing that Jesus would be dining with Simon the Pharisee, the woman grabbed her most prized possession and made her way to the prestigious gathering. In that culture citizens of a town frequently crowded around the walls or portals of homes where large events took place. Occasions such as Simon's reception would have been a main attraction in the day. Typically held in the large dining rooms or the lush courtyards of the upper class, events like this boasted guest lists that included only the most influential. Just as in our day people stand along sidewalks to get a glimpse of Hollywood's glamorous few, so was the custom then. The doors of Simon's home swung open to anyone who wanted to glimpse into the lives of the rich and famous.

On this high-profile night, the topic of discussion likely centered on theology. Jesus' reputation as a powerful teacher of the Law had spread rapidly in the region. What an opportunity for a "town hall meeting" between the young, radical rabbi from Nazareth and the respected Pharisee Simon. For the common citizens of the town, an event like this was an exciting affair in their pre-television, pre-let's-go-to-the-movies world.

So for this woman to be among the onlookers at the dinner struck no one as unusual.

That is, until she stepped through the crowd and inched toward Jesus. You can be sure the room grew silent. The clattering of dinnerware and the chattering of busy servants stopped, side conversations at the table became irrelevant, and the buzzing among the onlookers trailed off into whispers. All eyes were fixed on her. Everyone knew who she was and how she lived. She was "a sinner" (v. 39 NIV). As she stepped into the space reserved for the invited guests, a chill must have hit the room. Simon the Pharisee sat stunned. The evening was not going as he had planned.

What she did next not only stole the show but defied all tradition. She continued to make her way to Jesus. Finding Him, she stopped at His feet—where the servant of the house would normally stand—and broke into sobs so deep they released a stream of tears onto the Master's feet. She loosened her hair to wipe His feet, then bowed to kiss them over and over again. As she opened a vial of alabaster and anointed His feet, a heavy, alluring fragrance permeated the room.

Simon was scandalized! Before the meal, he would have performed ritualistic cleansings to purify himself according to the traditions of the code of the Pharisees. For a woman —and particularly a woman of such ill character—to lovingly anoint Jesus in the presence of Simon and his guests violated all sense of religious propriety. It simply wasn't done. Such a bold and beautiful expression of love was incomprehensible coming from someone so obviously unfamiliar with the religious constructs of "goodness."

A rare courage and refreshingly innocent audacity marked her remarkable act of sacrificial love.

Her adoration in plain view of the crowd forced Jesus into a predicament. The crowd's attention had been riveted on the woman; now it suddenly turned to Simon's honored guest. What would He do? After all, His host, proud Simon, held all the power. He set the standards for what was publicly acceptable and what was not. This woman had crossed the boundaries of religious and moral propriety. Jesus risked marginalizing Himself and offending His pompous host if He accepted her. He knew that the religious leaders had already repudiated His teaching. Now they'd have solid proof of His fondness for sinners.

Let's be honest. It's hard to do what is right when we're under pressure to play to the powerful and privileged among us. We love that kind of approval. Who among us would not have wanted to be accepted by the prestigious group reclining at Simon's table? Jesus could have easily capitalized on the situation. By casting His lot with the power broker Simon, He might have gleaned an endorsement that would have given His ministry a boost.

But, Jesus resisted all that. Without hesitation, He affirmed her outpouring of love and became her Defender and Friend. One thing is clear: The woman's response to Jesus, though radical and culturally abhorrent, touched His heart. Beneath the layers of sin and unspeakable shame, Jesus sensed her stunning faith. Her sacrificial love demonstrated a heart filled with gratitude spilling out onto the One who loved her first. Jesus responded as a merciful Advocate of thankful souls who express genuine love for Him regardless of the cost. He proved that He is indeed a friend of sinners!

What gave rise to the radical and risky expression of love for Jesus that came from this unlikely person? And why was it so easy for such an unrighteous individual to show authentic love for Him and so hard for self-righteous Simon to do so? As we seek answers to these questions, we'll discover what we need in our lives to move from empty religion into an authentic relationship with Christ.

This chapter taken from Why It's Hard to Love Jesus, *Moody Publishers, 2003*

S imon sat stunned and offended as the woman clung to Jesus' feet. Though
he didn't speak, his thoughts betrayed his heart. Luke writes, "When
the Pharisee who had invited him saw this, he said to himself, 'If this man were
a prophet, he would know who is touching him and what kind of woman she
is—that she is a sinner'" (Luke 7:39 NIV).

Luke couldn't resist the irony. Jesus didn't have to hear Simon speak in order
to know his heart. He was a prophet. Luke simply wrote, "Jesus answered him,
'Simon, I have something to tell you'" (v. 40 NIV).

Jesus went on to explain the woman's behavior by telling Simon a story of
two debtors. One owed a great deal to a moneylender and the other owed con-
siderably less. Neither of them could repay, so the lender graciously forgave their
debts. Jesus asked Simon if he knew which debtor would love the moneylender
more—the one who was forgiven much, or the one who was forgiven little?
Simon responded, "I suppose the one who had the bigger debt canceled" (v. 43
NIV). Jesus affirmed Simon's correct response, then went directly to His point.

In a withering reproof, He confronted Simon's lack of genuine love. Simon had not extended to Jesus even the most common courtesy granted a guest—foot washing. Nor had he greeted Jesus with the customary kiss. Those acts of courtesy were like my asking you if I might hang up your coat if you were to come to our home in Chicago in the dead of winter. For me not to ask to hang up your coat would imply an unwelcome response to your visit. As we will see, there might have been reasons for Simon to withhold these routine gestures of hospitality, but in this cultural setting his actions would be rude and offensive to any guest, let alone Jesus.

Jesus hadn't missed the snub. In addition to withholding the common courtesies of the day, Simon had denied Jesus the grace of being refreshed with oil. Ordinarily, when guests of honor arrived, they'd be given a special anointing of oil to freshen their faces. Poorer families offered less expensive fragrances for the ritual. Pharisees, on the other hand, anointed their guests with the finest products, demonstrating their prestigious positions in the community. Simon had done none of that.

He hadn't felt it appropriate to honor Jesus with an anointing. Yet this despised woman of the streets washed His feet with her tears and never stopped kissing Him. More remarkably, she brought the most expensive of oils to anoint His travel-weary feet.

Where did her outpouring of love come from? In essence Jesus explains that she was loving Him with such bold affection because she had been forgiven of great sin. Then, for Simon's benefit, He concluded, "But he who has been forgiven little loves little" (Luke 7:47 NIV).

Like the debtor in the parable Jesus told, the woman at Christ's feet loved much because she had been forgiven much. Nowhere in Scripture do we find that loving Christ is the reason for forgiveness. True expressions of love for Him flow as a spontaneous and unstoppable response to forgiveness. Acts of authentic love are a response to Christ's amazing work of grace. It is just that simple. Those who have been forgiven much, love much.

This sinful woman responded to Jesus with a deep and moving love because she belonged to a particular class of people . . . the forgiven much. Those of us who find ourselves in this class live lives fueled by the energy of a deeply indebted desire to express our gratitude through acts of adoring love for Christ. Genuine love for Him is always a response to His extreme grace extended to us.

~&

I wonder what sermon Jesus had preached at this point in His ministry that so deeply impacted the woman's heart. Unfortunately, Luke does not tell us what she heard or saw. But somewhere, at some time, Jesus touched her heart. He met her deepest need, delivering her anguished, exiled soul from fear and despair. Personally, I think Luke hints at when she first encountered Jesus. Earlier in this same chapter, Luke records that about this same time, John the Baptist had sent his disciples to verify Jesus' credentials (Luke 7:18–28). Matthew records those very events in his gospel and clues us into what sermon Jesus preached shortly after John's disciples left Him. And it was a life-changing message indeed!

Stand with this sinful woman in the crowd on that day when the region buzzed with excitement about the arrival of this country preacher from Nazareth. She had heard, perhaps even from a client, about this Jesus who healed the sick and restored sight to the blind. She may have heard, as strange as it would seem to her, that He had proven to be a friend of searching sinners. Coming to join the crowd—for she would have a Zacchaeus type of curiosity (Luke 19:1– 4)—she might have strained to see Jesus and hear His voice. She might have caught a glimpse of His face—a face unlike any she had seen before. Imagine the scene on that green, fruited hillside as it sloped lazily toward the Sea of Galilee. But it is Matthew who records the sermon she most likely heard on that day. Words from heaven like lightning bringing rays of light to her dark and threatened heart.

"Come to me, all you who are weary and burdened, and I will give you rest. Take my yoke upon you and learn from me, for I am gentle and humble in heart, and you will find rest for your souls. For my yoke is easy and my burden is light." *Matthew 11:28–30 (NIV)*

Think of what it would mean for this woman to hear such a welcoming, forgiving, merciful invitation. It was she who offered rest to men, in encounters that only left her more laden with guilt. No one offered her rest. No one cared for her soul. Men used her as an object of desire, only later to ruthlessly discard and condemn her. Any sense of worth and self-esteem was nonexistent in her abused and broken life. She lived under a burden of inextricable guilt, weighed down by the sludge of sin that polluted her soul. No one needed to tell her how lost she was. She lived with that condemning awareness daily. What she needed was someone to tell her that there was a way out, a way to be forgiven.

And now, for the first time in her life, this desperate woman had come into contact with a man who offered forgiveness and a love she could wholly trust. She must have seen something different in His face. He hadn't offered the looks of sly desire she had seen on the faces of so many other men. She sensed that she could feel safe with Him. Had she finally found someone who cared—someone who wanted, not to use her, but to honor and forgive her?

Later, as the crowd dispersed, she may have lingered to ask about the invitation He gave to anyone who would believe. Could it be that she qualified? Did He really understand who she was? Did it matter—as it had for most of her life? Surprisingly, He was willing to talk with her. His look and His voice raised her hopes that she might find grace in His sight. She heard what for her were almost unbelievable words. Unlike what she had been taught all her life, she heard that God offers mercy and grace and delights in forgiving those who come to Him seeking forgiveness and restoration.

She knew in a heartbeat that this was not only what she wanted but also what she needed. For too long she had been the object of men's lusts. Now she glimpsed an opportunity to become the object of a divine, redeeming love. And in a moment of unqualified belief, the sludge that had for so long clogged her soul with guilt and self-incrimination melted away in the cleansing flood of His forgiving grace. The fresh Spirit-breathed sweet air of forgiveness filled and healed her battered soul.

Is it any wonder that when she heard Jesus was dining at the Pharisee's home, she said, "I have to go and see Him once again—to tell Him how much I love Him!" Making her way through the streets that used to be the dark passages of her trade, she set out to express a new kind of love unstained by the past. Arriving at Simon's house, she may have been shocked by the rudeness shown to the Master. And without giving it another thought, she broke from the margins of the room, kneeled before Him, and worshiped Him with loving acts that far exceeded even the most careful courtesies Simon could have extended to Jesus.

Why? Because she was among the forgiven much. What she did in those moments reflected a moving and instructive response to redeeming love.

For her, as it must be for all of us, adoring expressions of love for Him spring from the life-liberating love He first gives us. He had stunned her heart with His marvelous forgiving grace, and now she responded in gratitude with courageous, reciprocal acts of love.

Mark it down: Loving Christ is a *response*—a response to His enduring, unwarranted love for us. His amazing grace motivates us like nothing else to live out our lives in unique and courageous ways that express our deep affection and honor for Him before a watching and often critical world. Why would you or I forgive a parent who had abused us? Why would we give generously to empower the work of Christ? Why do we serve as ushers or sing in the choir? Why would you feed the homeless or take dinner to a sick neighbor?

Why would anyone endure a difficult marriage out of conviction that it is the right and honorable thing to do? Why do Sudanese Christians permit themselves to be sold into slavery rather than deny the name of Christ? Why do people leave lucrative and prestigious positions to take lesser tasks in the kingdom work of Christ? Why have martyrs gladly died and others lived in terrible situations with bold, uncompromising spirits? Believe me, such rare selflessness does not arise out of a sense of obligation. Commitment to duty does not provide sufficient resolve. When the chips are down or the stakes are high, mere commitment rarely works.

Since He has lovingly done so much for us, genuine lovers of Christ move quickly from a religion expressed through empty routine to a love marked by unstoppable gratitude. Authentic lovers of Jesus thrive on opportunities to express their love to Him as a living response to His grace.

So if you truly desire to be that kind of Christ-lover you must ask, "Where am I on the continuum between the Pharisee and the immoral woman?" Allow the Holy Spirit to probe your past. When was the last time you were willing to do something radical and dramatic to express your overflowing love for Jesus? Is there a momentum in your soul that pushes toward a deepening, life-altering love for Him, or are you stuck in the cognitive and bound by a codified, passionless arrangement with Him? The answers to these questions determine the authenticity and integrity of your and my claim to love Jesus.

To love Christ—to really love Him—means that, like the sinful woman, we intentionally seek ways to express our love clearly and without intimidation, regardless of the cost. It is gratitude toward a forgiving and grace-extending Savior that drives us to seek out ways to say, "Thank You! This is how much I love You."

⌁

Where did Ruth McBride—broken by life and its deep disappointments—get the powerful resolve to live above the brokenness? She found the genuine item in the only One who could fill the gaping hole life had left in her soul. Her life had been dramatically changed by Christ.

She had one regret. What really bothered Ruth Jordan McBride was her deep guilt for not having gone to be with her mother before she died. While it was true that her family had officially rejected her and refused to tell her where her mother was, Ruth blamed herself for deserting her mom and deeply grieved the lack of closure. Her son recounts Ruth's own words in his book about her life.

~&

I was depressed for months. I lost weight and couldn't eat and was near suicide. I kept saying, "Why couldn't it have been me that died?". . . Dennis was the one who shook me out of it. He kept saying, "You've got to forgive yourself, Ruth. God forgives you. He'll forgive the most dreaded sin, the most dreaded sin." But I couldn't listen, not for a long while, I couldn't listen. I was so, so sorry. Deep in my heart I was sorry. . . . Lord, I was burning with hurt . . . I didn't think she was dying when I left home, but she knew it. . . . All her life I was the one who translated for her and helped her around, I was her eyes and her ears in America, and when I left . . .well, . . . her husband treated her so bad and divorced her, and her reasons for living just slipped away. It was a bad time.

It took a long time to get over it, but Dennis stuck it out with me, and after a while I began to listen to what he said about God forgiving you and I began to hold on to that, that God will forgive you, will forgive the most dreaded sin.[1]

~&

When Ruth realized that God had lifted the burden of her sin by bearing it Himself on the cross, she turned her eyes and heart toward Him as Savior,

Redeemer, Liberator, and Friend. She never recovered from the impact of His love. And she never stopped gratefully expressing it to Him in sacrificial acts of love lavished on an untidy brood of kids whose lives now bless thousands of people.

Ruth lived out her life in the face of great odds as a member of that select group of those who have been forgiven much. Her response flowed out of a passionate love for Christ. Her love for Him saw her through the darkest days.

Charles Wesley's timeless hymn "And Can It Be That I Should Gain" catches perhaps better than any other the sentiment of lives lived in the realm of the forgiven much. The sinning woman of Luke 7 and the countless Ruth McBrides of this world might join in grateful chorus in such rare expressions of gratitude and praise. The question is . . . can you?

> Long, my imprisoned spirit lay
> Fast-bound in sin and nature's night;
> Thine eye diffused a quick'ning ray,
> I woke, the dungeon flamed with light;
> My chains fell off, my heart was free;
> I rose, went forth, and followed Thee
> Amazing love! How can it be?
> That Thou, my God, shouldst die for me!

This chapter taken from Why It's Hard to Love Jesus, *Moody Publishers, 2003*

D oes the name Josh Gibson ring a bell?

Many of us remember several years back when, in a world short on heroes, major-league baseball served up a home run competition that pitted Cardinals muscleman Mark McGwire against Cubs superstar Sammy Sosa. All of America watched as the two vied day after day to break one of sports' most coveted records. They both surpassed Babe Ruth's 60 home runs, and then flew by Roger Maris' claim of 61 before McGwire pulled away and took the prize with 70 homers.

Enter Mr. Gibson. In all the hullabaloo over the Sosa-McGwire duel; in all of the reflections on the life and history of past record holders Ruth and Maris, there was hardly a mention of Josh Gibson. The omission is noteworthy. Gibson is considered by many as the greatest power hitter ever to hold a bat in any baseball league in the United States. He played from 1930 to 1946. In the 1931 season, at the age of 19, he hit 75 home runs in one season, a feat that no one has ever even approached.

Perhaps the reason that Gibson is an unsung hero is that he played mostly in what was known as the Negro League. His record was set at a time when, due to fear and ignorance, blacks and whites could not play in the same league. And, for any who might think this other league was inferior, we should realize that Negro League teams played against the white teams hundreds of times and compiled a three-to-one winning average against them.

According to some accounts, Gibson hit a staggering 962 home runs in his 17-year career and compiled a lifetime batting average of .391. In 1972, he was inducted posthumously into the National Baseball Hall of Fame.

I wouldn't have known of Josh Gibson except for an e-mail sent by an African-American to several friends. He started the note by saying: "Please share with your children, grandchildren, and brothers and sisters everywhere . . . the home run record has not been broken!" He went on to detail the stellar career of Gibson and to extol his athletic virtues. He wanted to set the record straight and to let the world know who the home run hero really was!

I then found my mind racing to the unsung hero of our hearts, Jesus Christ. Lost in the clutter of a world consumed with lesser things, our Lord and His unsurpassed accomplishments not only go unnoticed, but are often unwelcomed by many who do not want to know—lest they become morally accountable to someone besides themselves.

This fear and ignorance is not unlike the resistance that forced Christ to live and work outside the arenas where others strutted their stuff to advance their own causes and serve their own agendas. I'm reminded of a bittersweet Christmas song that both celebrates His birth and foreshadows His death: "Sweet little Jesus boy . . . we didn't know who you was."

As followers of Christ, it is our privilege to become advocates of the most accomplished person who has ever lived. Like my friend who was compelled to remind his world of Josh Gibson, we ought to be ready and willing publicists for the King of Kings. The spectacularly gracious works of our Savior and friend were never intended to be treasures that we hoard for our own enjoyment. His goodness is meant to be a testimony to a watching world of the reality of His power and personal care of all those who trust Him.

The psalmist wrote: "God be gracious to us and bless us and make his face shine upon us, that your ways may be known on earth, your salvation among all nations . . . and God, our God, will bless us . . . and all the ends of the earth will fear him" (Psalm 67:1–2, 6–7 NIV).

Opportunities to communicate the reality of God's greatness abound. When others recognize some obvious blessing in our lives, it is a prime moment to turn the spotlight on Him. We should make known answers to prayer, giving God the full credit. The most powerful statement of all is the witness of a transformed life. When they ask why we are different, then their hearts are ready to hear of our God.

This chapter taken from Moody *Magazine, January/February 1999*

A letter arrived from a woman I had pastored some years ago in Detroit. Mary wrote to tell me her dad had passed away. I loved her dad. He was a quiet, deep man whose life I held in the highest regard. It was easy to respect Larry. Most who knew him felt the same way. Most significantly, his family felt that way. Larry and his wife moved to Louisville to retire near one of their married daughters. Over a period of time, three of his daughters and their husbands moved to live near them. As one of the sons-in-law said, Larry was so special that he wanted his four children to grow up knowing him. Larry died of a cancerous brain tumor. As he became ill, the men cared for him. They counted him their best friend.

Mary wrote that even though her dad became quite immobile toward the end, he still knelt before God in prayer each night. It took two people to get him back on his feet again and into bed. Though he knew little else, he still knew his Savior.

Larry had walked the streets of Detroit during the riots of the '60s ministering to those who were injured. His love for people, especially the downcast, led him to encourage Mary to take a job teaching in the inner city sixteen years ago. He never had a high profile, at least not with men. But Larry had an enviable, visible, and contagious love for others—and for Christ. Mary writes, "I remember him as an energetic man who had no fear to do what was right in the eyes of God."

What struck me in the letter was what a friend said at the funeral. "It hurts so much because the world has lost a righteous man, and that is no small thing." I have often wondered what they will say about me when I am gone. What friends and family say is a commentary on the legacy we leave behind. Most of us have been so busy building a life that we have forgotten that life is really about building a legacy. To watch most of us, you would think we are hoping they will say something about our busyness, our accumulation of stacks of stuff, our travels, our golf, our detailed knowledge of every sport statistic known to man, or our computer wizardry. It's a commentary on our times that body-building gets higher billing these days than legacy building.

Some of us do far better in growing a career than a legacy. As my friend Howard Hendricks says, "You spend your life climbing the ladder of success only to find that when you reach the top, it is leaning against the wrong wall." Think of standing at the threshold of eternity and looking back at your life. What would you like the spin to be? What would the sound bites say? Would the phrases surround words like *godly, wise, caring, compassionate, honest, courageous,* and *Christlike?* Would they talk about how much we had loved our spouses and made our children a priority? Would they have noticed that we loved Christ more than anything else in life . . . that we had lived a life that reflected all we said we believed?

Are any of us living a life that is so solidly compelling that our kids want to be sure that our grandchildren don't miss letting us rub off on them? Mary's letter reminds me that my life needs to be about giving those who are left behind the summary of a life whose memories cast a long, powerfully positive shadow over the generations to come.

⁓

I'd give anything if they could say of me, "It hurts because the world has lost a righteous man, and that's no small thing." And that may be what I have to give . . . anything that gets in the way of my being a righteous man who, as Mary said, "had no fear to do what was right in the eyes of God." In my book that's a legacy worth leaving—and worth living for.

This chapter taken from Moody *Magazine, January/February 1999*

Remember those "Baby on Board" yellow window stickers? They warned other drivers that tucked inside those huge machines of plastic, aluminum, and steel, hurtling down the freeways, was perhaps a precious, valuable, vulnerable baby. They were popular—and, of course, their popularity gave rise to a host of other signs: "Ex-boyfriend in trunk!" "Nobody on board!" Fun. But then, in response to the original "Baby on Board" sign came the reply, "Who cares?" When I saw those I thought, How cold can you get? Who cares? Who cares about a precious baby on board? Maybe it was intended as humor, but it was callous nonetheless.

As I thought about that sign, its spiritual application penetrated my heart like a spear. I thought about those things that are precious to God. I thought about those who are vulnerable in this fast-moving, hell-bound world. I thought about the lost—those who don't know Jesus Christ—and about how precious they are to God. Then I wondered if God looks at my life—even though I'm busy around the kingdom—and sees a big, yellow diamond swinging from my neck that says, "Who cares? Who cares?"

~&~

One of the problems in our secularized world is that the worth of an individual is founded on his or her performance. Whether in relationships, business, entertainment, or athletics, the people who perform the best supposedly have the most worth. Conversely, those who are unproductive or underachieving have little worth. And, as Christians we can easily impose this notion on those who reject Christ, especially those who are blatantly evil. Who cares what happens to them? They deserve their fate!

God, however, tells us that *all* people have worth in this world—and that includes the lost. When God looks at this world, He attaches great value to the lost. Somehow, we must reclaim the roots of an authentic Christianity, which reminds us of that. We need to hear God's heartbeat, change the way we think about the lost, make decisions that will rip the "who cares?" sign from our necks, and begin to extend ourselves compassionately to those around us who need Jesus Christ.

In Luke 15 three famous episodes vividly illustrate this point. Here we are reminded that we are not the only ones who have struggled with one of those apathy signs. In this chapter Christ tells the stories of the lost coin, the lost sheep, and the lost son (better known as "the prodigal son").

As we examine these stories, we need to remember that Jesus Christ never told stories just to entertain a crowd. When Christ told a story, He told it to make an important point. The point of these stories, in fact, goes straight to the heart of the commission Christ gives us concerning the lost.

In addition, when Jesus Christ told a story, He based it in a setting or a context. Therefore, we will not understand these three stories until we understand the tension out of which they developed.

So we read in Luke 15:1, "Now all the tax collectors and the sinners were coming near Him to listen to Him." Notice the order in which the people are mentioned. In Christ's day, the tax-gatherers were despised turncoats—Jewish by birth, but they had sold out to Rome. The Roman authorities expected them to collect a tax of a certain percentage from the Jewish people, but they were also free to collect any additional fees they chose. In short, it was government-approved extortion. In the Jewish mind, tax collectors were the dregs of society. In this context, Jesus Christ was standing in the center of a crowd—maybe in the marketplace or in the outer courts of the temple. As the crowd gathered around Him, along came the tax collectors.

The "sinners" were also gathering around Christ. "Sinners" is a technical term in New Testament terminology that refers to people who basically had no regard for righteousness or the law of God. They lived as if God did not exist. They had no accountability but simply did whatever they wanted. Unlike in our society, Judaism in that day regarded the law of God and His righteousness as the standard, which meant that "sinners" also were among the lowest people in Jewish culture.

The text tells us that all the tax-gatherers and all the sinners were coming near to listen to Him. As the episode opens, Christ is at the core of this crowd of lost people, who were not just the socially-acceptable lost—as in our day—but the *really* unacceptable.

So who would be the "worst" for us as believers today? Abortion providers? Drug addicts? Homosexuals clamoring for the right to "marry"? The liberal media that seem so intolerant of biblical faith? Immoral celebrities?

The issue is, do we care about them? Do we pray for them and seek ways to win them to Christ? They too are in need of a Savior.

❦

Verse 2 continues to build the tension: "And both the Pharisees and the scribes began to grumble." Picture the scene: Christ is at the center of the crowd, and as the tax collectors and sinners begin to press toward Him, the "religious" people of the day, the Pharisees and the scribes, come along. They say, "This man receives sinners and eats with them." In other words, "He spends His time with the worst of the lost!"

Why was this such a problem to the Pharisees and the scribes? Because Jesus Christ had claimed to be God, and like some religious leaders today, the scribes and Pharisees wanted to condemn Him for hanging around with the ungodly. This Man who claimed to be God spent time with "terrible people."

That attitude is similar—if not identical—to the wrong thinking of many Christians today. The religious leaders' theology was a "good guys/bad guys" theology. Their thinking was that because God was good and perfect, His representatives and His Messiah would hang around only with those who were a part of the "good guys' club." Who did they think were the good guys on earth? Themselves, of course! They assumed that because God is a holy God, those tax collectors and sinners would surely be judged and condemned by Him. Such people were therefore unworthy of time and attention. Therefore, they reasoned that if Christ were really God, He'd be walking around with the religious crowd, reproving the lost from a distance and pronouncing judgment on them. Instead, this Man who claimed to be the Messiah fraternized with the lost, and that made no sense!

❦

But God's heart for the lost does make sense if we put God into each of these stories—and think about the fact that *God Himself has suffered a significant loss.*

Consider, for example, a shepherd who had only a hundred sheep. In

Christ's day a shepherd's flock was his bank account. If a shepherd lost even one of his sheep, he suffered a significant loss.

If a widow has only one small bag of coins to support her through the end of her life and loses one coin, she has suffered a significant loss.

And what about a father who has lost a wayward child? What could be a more significant loss? God cares for the lost because He Himself has suffered a significant loss – the loss of something dear to Him.

Let's put this into the context of Scripture. In Genesis 1–2 we read that God created all things and then stood back and said, "That's good." The pinnacle of that creation was man and woman, whom He created to have fellowship with Him. He created them in His image so that they could know Him and so that His character could flow through them. They would demonstrate to all creation what the invisible God is like.

But in Genesis 3, sin enters and rapes the scene, leaving mankind dead in trespasses and sins and hopelessly alienated from God. That's when God suffered a significant loss because of sin. When Adam and Eve sinned, He could have just vaporized His creation and started over again. But He didn't. Instead, He went back to the Garden and called to Adam and Eve. Once He exposed their sin, He set the precedent of sacrifice to cover sin and redeem that which was lost.

The rest of Scripture, then, is about the way God has chosen to bring the lost back to Him again. It reveals to us how the nation of Israel carries the seed of Messiah. It gives us the history of that seed protection and His arrival at the cross, the empty tomb, and the resurrection. When we get to the end of the Bible, we find a new heaven and a new earth in Revelation 21. Because of the redemptive work of God, we who believe will all be with Him together. John heard a loud voice say, "God will dwell among them, and they shall be His people, and God Himself will be among them" (v. 3). That which He lost at the Fall will be regained! So great was God's loss that it has preoccupied the entire flow of history. It is of eternal concern to Him. It was the first crisis revealed in Scripture, and it is the last to be resolved. God cares for the lost because when man died in sin God suffered a personal loss.

Many of us have suffered significant losses: a spouse, a parent, a child, a close friend. We know how greatly that hurts. We say, "If I could only have him back!" If that is how we feel, imagine the heartbeat of God, who has lost His creation to sin and how greatly He desires to win them back.

~&

These stories also demonstrate the proof that God cares. What is that proof? It is that He was willing to intervene.

The lost are hopelessly, helplessly lost without Him. The shepherd lost his sheep, and that lamb was hopelessly lost until the shepherd intervened. Sheep are not quite up to par mentally. Lambs don't come home by themselves. In fact, if you put them out to pasture, they'll eat the pasture down to the dirt. And if they don't have a shepherd to lead them on or take them home, they'll die of starvation in that dry pasture. Whoever gave Little Bo-Peep that famous advice led her astray. "Leave them alone and they'll come home, wagging their tails behind them." She, no doubt, is still waiting.

Even the prodigal son would have remained utterly lost if his father hadn't forgiven him. Many people think the great offense of this story is that the boy spent all his money in riotous living. But that's not the point of the story at all. The point is the son's tremendous offense against his father.

First, he asked for his inheritance ahead of time. In the Middle Eastern culture, even today, if a child does such a thing, it's as though he were saying to his father, "I wish you were dead."

Second, in addition to insulting his father, he cashed out his assets and left for a foreign land. He took his portion of the estate, his dad's personal social security, and he wasted it all on selfish living. He brought shame to his family. Then he ended up working on a Gentile pig farm. What was a nice Jewish boy doing in such a place like that? If we properly understand the Eastern mind-set when this story was told, we know that the Pharisees held no hope for that boy. They would never countenance a father's forgiving a son who behaved the way this prodigal son did. Such a boy would have no hope unless his father intervened and forgave him.

This does away with all the nonsense we hear to the effect that we're not really dead in sin, just "wounded." All we have to do is get up, pull ourselves up by the bootstraps, think positively, and get going. But God's Word makes abundantly clear that we are dead in our trespasses and sins. Unless there is some intervention from God, we are hopelessly and helplessly lost.

God cares because He has suffered a loss, and He has proved that He cares by choosing to intervene on behalf of those who are helplessly lost. That is why Jesus Christ was at the center of that crowd. That is why Jesus Christ hung on the cross and shed His blood. That is why the Father touched Christ's tomb and brought Him to life, proving that He can give life to all who come to Him, cling to the cross, and receive the Savior for themselves.

These stories tell us that all the lost have worth to God—every one of them. We've already talked about what a sheep means to a shepherd, what a coin means to a widow, what a son means to a father. Look around you. Look at the businessman who keeps cheating you with contracts that are dishonest while you're trying to live with integrity. God cares for him. Look at the relative who keeps offending you, even though you're extending love and concern. God cares for her. Every sinner in this world has value to God.

When Christ told these stores, He depicted things of inherently high value to the persons who had lost them: a sheep, a coin, a son. Today we can apply that principle to people in our culture who seem beyond salvation: godless judges, disease-ridden prostitutes, prisoners sentenced for life, purveyors of pornography. God sees all of these lost ones as having worth.

～&

Christ told these three stories not only to prove that if God were here, He'd be right at the core of the crowd with the lost; He told them to instruct those who say, "Who cares?"

God wants us to hate the darkness and fight its influences. But He also wants us to remember that trapped in the darkness are people precious to God— people we, too, should love.

Within these stories, then, we find profound truths concerning ways we might reorder our values in relation to the lost. Christ Himself speaks to our hearts, thoughts, and actions concerning all those for whom He died.

～&

The first practical lesson we can learn from these stories is that if we are to adopt God's agenda for the lost, we must *repent of our prejudices.*

Us? Prejudiced? Imagine yourself walking through a mall, and suddenly a group of teenagers approaches. They're wearing T-shirts bearing grotesque images. Their heads are shaved on one side, with green, yellow, purple, and red spikes coming out the other side. Their earrings dangle, and their leather wristbands have metal spikes on them. As they come toward you, what are you going to say? "Hi, gang, how are you doing today? Hope you have a wonderful time in the mall"? Or do you, as you walk by them as far away as possible, think, *Thank you, Lord, that I'm not like that?*

"Maybe we are prejudiced," you might argue, "but I've read this chapter of the Bible, and I don't see anything in it about prejudice." Actually, why are the Pharisees standing at the fringe of the crowd saying, "He spends time with people like that"? Because they have a problem with prejudice. And just as their prejudices built barriers among the people Christ cared for, so prejudices build barriers between us and those God loves through us. As soon as we start mentally segregating different kinds of people, saying,

"They don't have worth," we stop feeling the need to communicate Christ to them.

That is why Jesus Christ said God the Father is like a shepherd. In a Pharisee's mind, a shepherd was at the low end of the caste system – with the tanners, tax collectors, and prostitutes. Did you ever wonder why David didn't get invited when the prophet Samuel came to his family's house? Somebody had to watch the sheep, and since he was the youngest child in the family, the role of shepherd had been relegated to him – all the way at the bottom of the family ladder. Pharisees had a deep prejudice against shepherds. They were probably shocked to hear Christ indicate in the first story that "God is like a shepherd who has lost a sheep" (see Luke 15:3–7).

Similarly, the Pharisees had a low opinion of women. They viewed women as chattel, sources of defilement, sources of temptation, and the guilty parties in cases of adultery. If a Pharisee was walking along and saw a woman coming toward him, he would cross the road to avoid her. But Jesus said, "God is like a woman who lost a coin" (see vv. 8–10).

We have already discussed what a despicable offense the wayward son committed against his father. The Pharisees would have said that the father should never forgive that boy. So Jesus said, "God is like the forgiving father of a prodigal son" (see vv. 11–32).

In all three stories Christ uses a spirit of conviction to back our prejudices against the wall. We have to remember that in order to care for the lost, we first need to address the problem of prejudice that builds barriers between us and certain "others."

One of the most wonderful things about many of God's people today is a genuine concern about missions—the desire to reach the world for Christ. We're all into missions, it seems. But guess what's happening? In America today, the world is moving to our cities and to our neighborhoods. The mission fields are coming from all over the world to us. That sounds exciting … unless you live in a nice suburb, and suddenly your neighbor puts up a "For Sale" sign, sells the house, and four weeks later a big truck pulls up. As you look through the blinds, you notice that the people moving in aren't like you. They don't have the same ethnic background. They don't have the same color of skin. They may not even speak English very well.

What happens then to your zeal for missions? Do you say, "Fantastic! God has brought the mission field to my neighborhood! Now I can be a missionary"? Do you yell to your spouse, "Sweetheart, let's fall to our knees and start praying. We've been wanting to be missionaries all our lives, and now we get to do it"? It's doubtful. More likely, we turn to our spouse and say, "Well, sweetheart, do you know a good realtor?"

When I was a little kid in church, we used to sing a song that went like this: "Red and yellow, black and white, all are precious in His sight." Why did we stop singing that? Did we get too sophisticated? Or did that song get a little too convicting? We will go nowhere with the gospel until we look at every single person in our world as having worth to God. If we're going to think correctly about the lost, we need to repent of our prejudices.

⚓

Once we've repented of our prejudices, it is time to commit ourselves to being seekers of the lost. Let's look again at Christ's first story in Luke 15. The principles are rich. In fact, we can find four definite traits of a serious seeker of the lost.

In verse 4 Christ asks, "What man among you, if he has a hundred sheep and has lost one of them, does not leave?" First and foremost, seekers are *leavers*.

If we are ever going to be effective for the gospel, we've got to get out there with the "others" and rub shoulders with them. But also, seekers are *finders*—

like the shepherd who leaves the ninety-nine in open pasture and goes after the single lost sheep until he finds it. Unfortunately, some of us only make brief little forays into the other world: "I went out there," we say. "I saw five of them. They're really out there—no kidding! But I'm sure glad to be back! Whew, what an experience."

Third, in verse 5 we read that "when he has found it, he lays it on his shoulders." Seekers are *bearers.* At this point some of us are thinking, Whoa, time out! Do you mean to say that if I happen to lead a business associate to Christ, or a neighbor, or even a stranger, I need to bear him or her back to the safety of the fold? That's right. You mean I've got to invite him to that monthly potluck we've been going to for nineteen years with the same four couples? Ask him to sit with me in church? Follow up and help him make the transition from the habits of darkness to the principles and thoughts of the kingdom? Absolutely correct. Serious seekers are not only leavers and finders; they are bearers who take the precious lamb that's been found, put it on their shoulders, and bear it safely back to the fold.

Finally, if you are committed to being a serious seeker, you will not only be a leaver, a finder, and a bearer—you will also be a *rejoicer.* The shepherd returned rejoicing. In fact, Luke's particular literary approach underscores one grand theme—rejoicing. Why did Luke emphasize the theme of rejoicing? Because the scribes and Pharisees were murmuring and grumbling! Christ was saying emphatically that their prejudicial grumbling reflected the fact that they didn't have the heart of heaven.

ॐ

As I minister in churches across America, I have become concerned about some of our churches. It seems that many of our churches have been laid out, nailed shut, and buried six feet under. What has happened to our joy? What happened to our spirit of celebration? We are on the victor's side. We've been redeemed. But we have no joy. Where did it go?

There could be many reasons, but one thing is sure—there is a good chance that in a church without joy the lost haven't been sought for a long, long time. Conversely, if we begin to see a revival of caring for the lost and spending of time at the core of the crowd, we are going to be surprised at the joy that suddenly is infused into our congregations. Why? Because seekers are rejoicers.

When we first came to Chicago, we had four Sundays free. So we decided to visit several different churches on those open weekends. We went to a leading African-American Baptist church, and we sat through their service for a full two and a half hours. It was wonderful! The choir was terrific. The preacher preached a great message. And at the close of that message, he gave an invitation to take a public stand for Christ. The choir began to sing, and the congregation began to join the choir. They sang—but no one came forward. Then, after what I thought was quite an extended period of time, one man stood up in the back and started walking slowly down the aisle. Do you know what that congregation did? They broke out in spontaneous applause. I loved it! And I thought, *How much like heaven this is—when even one comes, all heaven rejoices.*

Before we moved to Chicago, we used to take our children to the museums in Chicago at Christmastime. And while we were in the city, we would do a little Christmas shopping, too. I will never forget the time when, in a huge multi-tiered mall, we suddenly looked around and discovered that our little boy Matthew was gone. He was probably about four years old at the time, and instantly, all the horror stories about little children being kidnapped in malls filled our hearts. Immediately, our assignment changed. No longer was it leisurely shopping. It was time to find the lost! That boy had phenomenal value to us, so we took up our assignment with zeal and urgency. I went out into the parking lot yelling, "Matthew! Matthew!" I felt like a total fool, but the cause was far more important than how I felt. I didn't find him. When I came back inside, Martie hadn't found him, either. Nor had my mother. But then we saw my dad walking down the aisle with little Matthew in hand—blond hair, glasses, smiling, and totally untraumatized. My dad had found him at the candy counter, standing there with his little hands behind his back, just looking at all the candy.

The interesting thing is that Matthew didn't *look* lost; but he was. He didn't know the grave danger he was in; but the peril was real.

You and I move about in a world where the people around us don't look lost and have no understanding of the eternal danger they are in. But their lostness is real, and the danger is acute.

We've been touched by His great love. Will we respond—and go seeking?

This chapter taken from The Dawn's Early Light, *Moody Publishers, 1990*

THREE

TAKE MY LIFE,
AND LET IT BE

K nowing more about me is not always a pleasant experience. Self-introspection often compounds my insecurities and doubts. Trips into my inner self often expose memories of past failures and resurrect fears of the future. That's why spending time getting to know Jesus is of such great value.

In fact, living to know Him is the key to understanding and making peace with ourselves. Trying to discover self-worth? You have it in Him—He died for you! Plagued by failure and guilt? He does what no one else will or can do for you—He forgives and forgets, kills the fatted calf as heaven rejoices, and clothes you with the best robes of His righteousness. Searching for significance? Search no more . . . you are His child. There is no greater significance than that. Trying to figure life out and wondering if there is any purpose for you to take up space on this planet? The mystery is unraveled in Him as He scripts your life to be lived for His glory and to reflect the reality of His character through your life. Let's face it, you'll never finally or fully make it on your own. Self

is forever inadequate to satisfy your soul and is inept to solve the restless searching of your heart.

But until we learn that lesson, we will continue to discover that the trouble
with self-focused living is that it is never resolved. Just when you think you know
all about yourself, you'll do something that surprises and disappoints you. Like
the gerbil, who spends considerable amounts of time running in his wheel, self-
absorbed people rarely get to resolution.

Life must be about more than getting to know ourselves. In fact if you are
determined to spend a great deal of time preoccupied with yourself, life is
bound to bore you to tears. None of us is that special.

Live to know Jesus.

This chapter taken from Strength for the Journey, *Moody Publishers, 2002*

Can We
Really
"Consider It
All Joy"?

One winter weekend, Martie and I decided to take one of those days we
rarely seem to have time for anymore. It was shortly after Christmas,
and our two oldest children had left for a trip with college friends. Our youngest
child, Matthew, was still at home, but he and two other friends had been looking forward all vacation to this particular Saturday. They were going to drive
three hours north to Wisconsin to go skiing.

Martie and I were delighted about the prospect of having an entire Saturday to ourselves. We would get up in leisurely fashion, make coffee, and sit
and chat. In the evening we were going to sit by the roaring fire as the snow fell
outside, put up our feet, read, and relax all by ourselves. It sounded delightful.

On Friday Matthew came to me and said, "Dad, we want to leave early
in the morning—at seven. So would it be OK if my two friends stayed overnight?" I said, "No problem."

However, he didn't tell me that these two friends had obligations Friday night. They came dragging in at 12:15 AM while we waited up to make sure everybody got in.

Then Matthew announced that he couldn't find his wallet. His two friends were not of driving age yet, so Matthew was supposed to do the driving the next day. We had to find that wallet. We looked all over the house, and he even drove back to a friend's house at 1:30 AM. But we could not find Matthew's driver's license. So I wrote a nice note for him to take: "To whom it may concern: This boy is my son, Matthew. He has my permission ... just last night he lost his wallet ... " and so on. He also had a certificate from his temporary license to take with him. At last we got everybody packed up and we went to sleep.

The next morning I woke up and looked outside. My driveway was a sheet of ice. I went down to the kitchen and said, "Boys, did you look outside yet?" "Yes." They looked at me with forlorn expressions as if to say, "You wouldn't tell us we can't go skiing after waiting all vacation for this day, would you?"

I'm a pushover, I admit. I said, "I'll tell you what I'll do. Just to be safe, let me drive out onto the main roads to see whether or not everything is OK." So I jumped into my car in my bathrobe, skidded down the driveway, and got onto the main streets. They were clear and smooth; everybody was moving at regulation speed. So about a quarter-mile down the street I started to turn around. I slowed down and then turned into a parking area—without noticing that it was sheer ice. My car started sliding, and my front right wheel hit the curb with all the weight of my car against it. It made a horrible noise. The only way I could keep the car going straight as I struggled home was to turn the steering wheel all the way in one direction. Somehow, I got the car to wobble into our driveway. Unfortunately, this was the car the boys had planned to take.

I walked inside and told the boys, "You're not going to believe this. I just wrecked my car." We had a second car, a Volkswagen Rabbit that was old and beat-up but relatively reliable. "We only have one option left," I said.

"If you guys want to go, you'll have to take the Rabbit." They groused about it, but finally they got everything inside the Rabbit, and off they went.

Finally, Martie and I were alone, though we were still a little concerned about whether the boys would make the trip safely. Halfway there, Matt called: "Dad, we made it this far, and everything's fine." I said, "Fine. An answer to prayer, Matthew. Keep driving safely." About another hour and a half went by, and I got another telephone call.

Matt said, "Dad, we're here."

"Oh, good. I guess everything went fine."

"Well, not exactly. About a mile and a half from the ski resort, the windshield wipers started slowing down, the radio stopped working, the lights started to dim, and finally they went out. Then the car quit. Some guy came along in a pickup truck and towed us up to the parking lot. What should I do?"

"Ask if there is a decent mechanic around. See if you can get his phone number, and I'll call him." So I called the mechanic, who said he'd look at the car, tow it back to the garage, and see if he could fix it. Two hours later, the mechanic called back to say the alternator had burned out and that he couldn't get a new one until Tuesday. After several unsuccessful attempts, we finally made contact with Matt and told him the car wouldn't be fixed until Tuesday. He said, "No problem, Dad. We found some friends who are here with their parents. They're staying in a motel about fifteen miles away, and their parents said we could stay in the room with them."

Later that night we got yet another telephone call from Matt. "We're here, Dad. In fact, when we checked in they had extra rooms, so I just got us our own room." I had given Matt my credit card "in case of emergency," so now this innocent little skiing trip was beginning to register dollar signs in my mind.

I said, "OK, Matt, fine. I'll pick you guys up tomorrow morning." The next day I drove seven hours round trip and brought the boys safely home.

End of story, right? Not quite.

The car was going to be ready Tuesday night. So Martie and I decided that Wednesday night after work we'd drive up to Wisconsin to pick up the car. As we were driving, however, I began to get tired, so I said, "Martie, would you drive for a while?"

She agreed. I pulled onto the shoulder of the interstate and opened the door—and just as I did, an eighteen-wheeler went screaming by. The wind shear caught the door and ripped it out of my hands. When I tried to shut it, I discovered that the door had been sprung. Need I say more?

⚘

I have a friend who says that the trouble with life is that it is "so daily." No matter who you are or where you are, trouble is inevitable. In Job we read that "man is born for trouble, as sparks fly upward" (Job 5:7). Not one of us is exempt.

Given that fact, we need to discover the truth about trouble. Our world likes to tell us that trouble is always unwelcome. In fact, we are told to do everything possible to avoid problems, pain, or crises that might come into our lives. The darkness we live in is more than willing to break up a home just because it is "troublesome" when life is not comfortable anymore. When the thought of children is "troublesome," we simply abort them. Francis Schaeffer was right when he observed that "the two things that Americans are into today are affluence and personal peace—personal peace meaning a life that is devoid of pain and trouble and grief."

But is that the way Christians should think? Admittedly, even Christians have been programmed to process trouble in terms of the priority of personal comfort at all cost. But if we are truly going to be set apart as unique lights in the ever-increasing darkness, we need to let God's wonderful, working, worthwhile Word change the way we think about and respond to trouble.

What, then, is the truth that can set us apart and make us different as we experience life's troubles? What is the truth about trouble?

The truth from God is that when trials come to us, they are used by God to make us, not break us. They are used to refine us, mold us, mature us, and conform us to the image of God's Son. That's God's truth about trouble.

James 1 outlines the process that leads to productive operational conclusions about crises and pain. We will see that again we have the opportunity to choose God's thoughts over the world's programming and make life decisions based on His conclusions, not our own.

The book of James begins, "James, a bond-servant of God and of the Lord Jesus Christ, to the twelve tribes who are dispersed abroad, greetings. Consider it all joy, my brethren, when you encounter various trials, knowing that the testing of your faith produces endurance. And let endurance have its perfect result, so that you may be perfect and complete, lacking in nothing" (vv. 1–4). The Phillips translation renders it, "My friends, when trouble enters your life, do not resist it as an enemy, but welcome it as a friend." Immediately it is clear that the advice from the Word of God is dramatically different from what our old, fallen natures and worldly culture tell us.

In this passage are several major dynamics that enable us to respond positively to trials, draw radically different conclusions, and practice God's truth about trouble in our daily decisions. Let's look at four major concepts and then focus on five facts that we can count on when trouble comes our way.

The first thing to note is the scope of this perspective on trouble. There are inconveniences: an unexpectedly expensive and chaotic ski trip falls into this category. There are tragedies: a lost spouse, a wayward child, broken homes, broken health. There's pain: severe disappointment with other people, dashed dreams, career losses.

What we need to understand from James 1 is that God's truth about trouble applies to us whether our troubles are as simple as a ski trip or as deep and devastating as the death of a loved one. How do we know that? Because the text says, "Consider it all joy, my brethren, when you encounter various trials." That literally means all kinds of troubles. From the smallest to the largest, from burned-up alternators to burned-out lives, God's Word tells us how we should think about each and every one.

Notice that this verse says, "*Consider* it all joy." It does not say that we should *feel* it a thing of joy when trouble enters our lives. We make a big mistake when we tell one another, "Feel joyful, no matter what. That's what James says." When we say that, we insinuate that true spiritual victory means walking through life with smiles on our faces regardless of the circumstances. We put people under tremendous pressure to be superficial and plastic about life, but we cannot expect them to show up at church beaming, even when their hearts are broken.

James does not command us to be any less or more than real people. Remember, even Jesus wept. Christ's heart was broken when He looked at the multitudes of Jerusalem who would not come to Him, and He shed tears when He stood at the tomb of Lazarus.

The word *consider* is borrowed from the accounting profession. It literally means to make a mental note of, to count, to consider, or to reckon on a ledger. It does not deal with how we feel but with how we think and respond. It tells us that when trouble rocks our lives, something needs to be reckoned in our brains. This affects the way we process information, draw conclusions, and make decisions. The one who "considers" is not concerned with changing the circumstances but with changing his or her attitudes and actions in the face of the circumstances.

What is the concept that needs to be "reckoned"? It is the radical thought that when trouble strikes, the circumstance—regardless of what it is—is worth thinking about from a joyful perspective. It is to be seen as a thing of joy, and we must honestly consider it that way. It is as though when trouble enters our lives we have numerous columns in which to tally the experience, just as an accountant has numerous columns in his ledger in which to make an entry.

There is, for example, a column called Blame. As trouble hits, we say, "I know what I'll do. I'll blame everyone around me for the problem." So we take our mental pencil and in our mental ledger put a checkmark under Blame.

There's another column called Self-pity. Trouble comes along, and we just feel sorry for ourselves. We throw a pity party. Of course, we don't invite anybody else to our pity party, because they'd wreck it. They'd try to cheer us up, or tell us it's not so bad. When trouble comes, many of us prefer to consider it unfair affliction.

Still others mark the ledger under the column of Bitterness, or Revenge. It's amazing how creative we can be in our revenge when someone causes us trouble. Since trouble often comes through unpredictable circumstances, we respond bitterly toward God Himself. Whether directed toward people or toward God, the Bitterness-Revenge column is often crowded with checkmarks.

While at a lunch with two leading Christian counselors, I asked, "What do you think the root problem is for most people who come in for counseling?" Without hesitation, each said that the most significant problem among Christians today is bitterness, either toward other people or toward God. That shouldn't surprise us. Hebrews 12:15 warns us to "see to it that no one comes short of the grace of God; that no root of bitterness springing up causes trouble, and by it many be defiled."

There are numerous other columns in our mental ledger. Some people have a well-used Unfair column, an Escape column, a Withdrawal column, or an Anger column. There are many, many ways we can consider, that is, think about, trouble when it enters our lives. But the Bible says that when it comes our way, we need to move all the way across the ledger to the Joy column and put a check there.

We may not feel joyful. In fact, that might even be an abnormal feeling for us to have. It might be hard for us to imagine or to understand how a particular episode could ever turn out to be something joyful. Yet the Bible says that mentally we need to consider it a thing of joy, knowing that its ultimate end will be positive.

The joy response cannot stand alone. It is possible only in relationship to what you know. Shortly after the bitter fighting at Gettysburg, the decisive Civil War battle which halted the progress of Robert E. Lee's mighty Army of Northern Virginia into Northern territory, Lee wrote to Confederate President Jefferson Davis: "We must expect reverses, even defeats. They are sent to teach us wisdom and prudence, to call forth greater energies, and to prevent our falling into greater disasters." Lee's response to adversity was informed by what he knew of the outcome of adversity. Our response to the setbacks of spiritual warfare should be no less sure.

James refers to this principle: "Consider it all joy, my brethren, when you encounter various trials, knowing . . ." (James 1:2–3). James made it clear to his readers that he wasn't talking about some kind of mental reckoning with no substance. It's not an empty promise of blind, shallow, fleeting joy. Rather, there are some things we can know for certain that enable us to consider it a thing of joy when trials and troubles come upon us. The Bible encourages us to use our minds to form certain conclusions that will change the way we react.

When we encounter trouble, many of us find that our minds tend to get a little fuzzy, and that clear thinking eludes us. Trouble – especially over the long term – tends to confuse us and confound our thinking processes. However, we can delight in the fact that in the midst of trouble there are some things we can always know; and the knowledge of those things enables us to count any trial or trouble a thing of joy.

If a doctor has ever told you that you needed surgery, it's unlikely that you responded by saying, "Oh, Doctor, that's wonderful! When you said that, I felt such a warm glow flow over me. Doctor, I feel so joyful about this! Can we do it right now?" Obviously not. When the doctor said, "Surgery," you probably thought, *This is going to hurt. I don't want any part of this.*

So why did you go through with the pain and trouble of surgery? What did you know ahead of time that enabled you to voluntarily put yourself through that agony? You knew that it would have a good final result. You knew it was something you needed. Perhaps you also knew that the doctor had a good reputation in this area or that someone else had undergone the same surgery with good results.

Regardless, the fact that you knew certain things enabled you to recognize that ultimately the surgery would be good for you. That enabled you to endure the trouble with patience, tranquility, and perseverance to "count" it a thing of joy.

The ancient Chinese had a unique mechanism for presenting their plays. They would present a play on a two-level stage. On the upper stage, the resolution of the drama was acted out as the story unfolded below. So as tension and mystery were building on the first level, the audience watching the resolution of the plot would yell to the people on the first level, "Hang in there! Don't give up! If you only knew!" What inspired that hope? It was the knowledge of what was happening on the second level.

I will never forget the 1980 Olympics hockey match between the U.S. team—composed of small, young, amateur players—and the Soviets. During the final period I was literally on the edge of my seat. I felt all the agony and anxiety of the contest as I watched it on television—and then suddenly we scored to go ahead late in the game! Can we hang on? I was tense, nervous, and traumatized. Our team went on to win, and I at last was ecstatic. Later that night the network broadcast a replay of the game, so I invited some friends over to watch it. I watched the same game again, but was I on the edge of my seat? Of course not. I sat back, propped up my feet, had a bowl of popcorn, and leisurely sipped Pepsi. I was watching the very same game—but what I knew about the outcome made a radical difference in my attitude and actions.

That's exactly what the Bible is telling us in James 1. We will never be able to respond to trouble biblically and to count it a joy until we know certain things. What are those things we can know? Let's look at five specific facts we can count on, which we can integrate into our thought processes whenever trials and troubles invade our lives. We can count on these as God's truth. And now is the time to learn them—not after our lives have been shredded by a crisis. It is extremely difficult to learn and implement these facts under the pressure and confusion of trials, so we should learn them while our minds are clear and we can commit them to our long-term memory.

⚓

The first thing we can know for sure is that God has supernatural options with which to help us that we have never dreamed of. Second Peter 2:9 tells us that the Lord knows how to rescue the godly from trials.

I find that many times when trouble comes my way, it's like being in a room with no windows and no doors. I feel like four dark walls are pressing in against me. To my mind, there are no possible solutions. Yet God knows exactly how He will deliver me.

Think of when the people of Israel were up against the formidable obstacle of the Red Sea. They had been delivered from Egypt by miraculous events but now had their backs to the water, with a horde of Egyptian soldiers bearing down on them. They reasoned, "God brought us out here into the wilderness to kill us. We would rather have been slaves in Egypt than to die out here" (see Exodus 14:10–11). But God had options they had never dreamed of. God knew how to deliver His people in time of trouble.

We can know that God already knows how He will deliver us. Even though we can't see them, He has supernatural options, and He will provide a way of escape.

⚓

The second thing we can know for certain is what I like to call the truth of "bearability." First Corinthians 10:13 tells us, "No temptation has overtaken you but such as is common to man; and God is faithful, who will not allow you to be tempted beyond what you are able, but with the temptation will provide the way of escape also, so that you will be able to endure it."

Though we usually think this verse is talking about temptation, its wording in the original language of the New Testament actually applies to all kinds of trials. God has not given us any trial or trouble that is not common to all people. Furthermore, He will not give us more than we can bear, and with the trial He will provide a way of escape. Remember this: if God permits trouble to come into our lives, we will be able to bear it. He promised He will not give us anything we cannot bear.

As the saying goes, "the God who knows our load limit limits our load." What kind of a Father in heaven would God be if He dumped trials and troubles on us that would crush and defeat us? First Corinthians 10:13 guarantees that all things that come our way will indeed be bearable. That is the truth of bearability.

Remember that God stands like a sentinel at the gate of our lives, and nothing moves through the gate without the divine, sovereign permission of God (Job 1). He weighs it all out. He knows us personally and intimately, and He permits nothing that we cannot bear.

~❧

Third, we can understand the great truth of God's support. We know from 2 Corinthians 12:7–10 that the apostle Paul struggled with a chronic difficulty he called his "thorn in the flesh." It was so much trouble to him, in fact, that he prayed three times that God would deliver him from it. If anybody had a direct pipeline in prayer, it was Paul. Yet God said no. God made clear to Paul that He had given that trouble to him so that in his weakness he would become strong in the Lord. Paul wrote, "And He has said to me, 'My grace is sufficient for you, for power is perfected in weakness.'" He went on to say that he was content with weaknesses: "For when I am weak, then I am strong." God's supporting grace made the difference for Paul. And God's supporting grace will make the difference for us.

In my years as a pastor, I have stood by people who went through incredible problems and deep pain. And most of the time, I found that they survived amazingly well. I would walk away thinking, *If that were me, I would have been a basket case.* Then I would remember the marvelous truth that when God permits trouble, He gives sufficient grace to supernaturally support us in our pain. According to 1 Peter 5:5 and Hebrews 12:15, the only way we can short-circuit God's grace in a time of trouble is to have a proud spirit or to become bitter. God gives grace. We know it and can count on it.

꘎

Fourth, we can know that God is willing to share His supernatural power with us in the midst of our problems. God supernaturally intervenes.

Some might blindly say, "I've had lots of problems, but I've never seen the power of God in them." If that's the case, perhaps we should think of all the power He has expended to eliminate those things that would have put us over the edge. Some nights, in fact, I go to bed praying, "Lord, I want to thank You for keeping me from those things I didn't even know about, things that would have totally done me in." That protection is the real power of God in my life.

Throughout Scripture, we see that God expends His divine, supernatural power for His people in the midst of problems. God is always the God of the possible. When the Lord reproved Sarah for her unbelief He asked, "Is anything too difficult for the Lord?" (Genesis 18:14). God is always willing to extend His supernatural power in His perfect timing for those who are in trouble.

⸰⸙

Finally, when we come face-to-face with trouble, we can know that it is a process with a purpose. "Consider it all joy, my brethren, when you encounter various trials, knowing that the testing of your faith produces endurance. And let endurance have its perfect result, so that you may be perfect and complete, lacking in nothing." God is never careless with us, His precious, blood-bought children. Any time He permits trouble and pain, it is always a process with a purpose.

Note what the purpose is: God wants us to be mature. He wants us to grow up to be like Jesus Christ. Biblical maturity is defined for us as coming into the measure of the fullness of Christ (Ephesians 4:13). That demands character, and problems forge character in our lives.

When I am just floating along with few problems, I find that I am much more vulnerable to forgetting how much I need God. I settle back into the groove of my self-sufficiency and think, *Maybe I'm OK just as I am.* On the other hand, troubles reveal what I'm like on the inside. Troubles reveal those things that need to be changed in my life in order for me to mature and to become more conformed to the image of Christ. And my troubles stimulate my devotion to Christ and my dependence on Him.

The trouble with trouble is that it exists. It always has, and it always will. "Man is born for trouble, as sparks fly upward" (Job 5:7). That's the trouble with trouble.

The truth about trouble is that God is greater. Therefore, we can triumph in trouble. He can cause us to see our troubles as a cause for ultimate joy, not debilitating grief. He gives us the divine perspective so that we might think clearly in the midst of trouble and draw operational conclusions that will produce godly decisions, decisions of forgiveness, patience, and productivity in the midst of pain. He will use trouble to make us more like His Son, Jesus Christ. What greater light could there be than to announce through our trials to a dark and troubled world that troubles don't break us but rather make us! Though we don't look forward to them, when they come we can welcome them as friends.

A doctor tells his patients, "This may hurt you, but I guarantee it will help you." Is that not the assurance of James 1? When our loving Great Physician allows the pain of trials and various troubles to enter our lives, He uses them to help us become "perfect and complete, lacking in nothing."

In a world addicted to comfort, peace, and convenience at any cost, when trouble embitters the human spirit, what a blaze in the night is the life that responds with confidence.

Yet another dynamic in response to trouble is yielding patiently to it. James 1:4 states, "Let endurance have its perfect result." Patiently yielding is strategic in the process.

Imagine the surgeon striding into the operating room, putting on his gloves, and suddenly noticing that the patient has leaped from the table. He can't effectively work on a moving, resisting target. Relax. Recognize God's goodness and ultimate purpose, and patiently trust His timing. Resist the urge to take everything into your own hands, to manipulate, to blame, to seek revenge and inflict pain. Remember He seeks to work on you. Yield to His purpose.

Then, pray. "If any of you lacks wisdom, let him ask of God" (James 1:5). As we consider trouble a thing of joy, based on what we know to be true, and as we yield to God's perfecting work, when we don't know what to do, we are to pray. This significant step focuses us away from the temporal pain and onto the character and directives of our eternally good Father. In prayer we are reminded of His goodness, His power, and His plans and principles. In prayer we sense His peace, which passes all understanding (Philippians 4:6).

Prayer puts it all in perspective. Prayer forces us to see our situation from His point of view. Prayer puts us face-to-face with our God. And as we see his brilliant character and glory, we will say with Job, "Though He slay me, I will hope in Him" (Job 13:15).

This chapter taken from The Dawn's Early Light, *Moody Publishers, 1990*

```
┌──────────────────────────────────────┐
│                                        │
│        F O U R T E E N                 │
│              ❧                         │
│          C u p   o f                   │
│     S w e e t n e s s ,                │
│          C u p   o f                   │
│        S o r r o w                     │
│                                        │
└──────────────────────────────────────┘
```

W ho doesn't love the "holiday" season?

Pressed into five quick and busy weeks are Thanksgiving, Christmas, and New Year's. Each comes with its own distinctive flavor, extended days off work, family, friends, festive music, an abundance of good food, and a little football. For those of us who know Christ, the celebrations take on a particularly profound meaning. Think of all we have to be thankful for because God sent His Son to be born, live, die, and rise so that all things could be made new. This string of holidays is like a metaphor of the significant realities in our lives.

Recently my wife, Martie, was reading through a small book on the 23rd Psalm that we picked up in a used bookstore in England. Its author is the prominent British pastor of the last century, F.B. Meyer. When he got to the phrase "My cup runneth over," his exposition was particularly moving. Meyer noted that all of us have cups of a different nature, some gold, some glass, some of earthenware. But Christ fills each cup with the same sweet and satisfying mixture of His grace. The reason that our cup is so abundantly full and sweet, Meyer explained, is because the cup that our Savior drank at the cross was so full of sorrow and shame.

"Consider the ingredients of Christ's cup—the shame and spitting; the pain and anguish; the physical torture … the bitterness of our sins, which were made to meet in Him; the guilt of our curse, which He voluntarily assumed; the equivalent of our punishment which was imputed to Him." Meyer went on to say it was as if "the human race stood in one long line, each with a cup of hemlock in his hands; and Christ, passing along, took from each his cup and poured its contents into the vast beaker which He carried: so that, on the cross, He 'tasted death for every man'" (Hebrews 2:9).

"Our cup is one of joy," said Meyer, "because His cup was one of sorrow. Our cup is one of blessedness, because His was one of God-forsakenness." Meyer continued, "Never forget the cost at which your brightest moments have been made possible." Meyer specified the bounty in our cup that we often take for granted: good health, friendships and love, comforts of home, the joys of the mind, and more. "Now and again there is a dash of extra sweetness poured into life's cup—some special deliverance; some unlooked-for interposition; some undeserved and unusual benediction—sent apparently for no other object than to satisfy God's passion for giving."

When Meyer got to this point, my heart was struck with the bountiful provision of our God. "But whatever blessing is in our cup it is sure to run over. With Him, the calf is always the fatted calf; the robe is always the best robe; the joy is unspeakable; the peace passeth understanding; the grace is so abundant that the recipient has all-sufficiency for all things, and abounds in every good work. There is no grudging in God's benevolence; He does not measure out His goodness as the apothecary counts his drops and measures his drams, slowly and exactly, drop by drop."

As Meyer notes, the greatest blessings in our cup are the mixture of spiritual joy, satisfaction, and peace in our communion with Christ. That sense of His full presence and the assurance of His power and protection in whatever life might hold for us is the greatest of all the blessings of God upon our lives.

Because our cups do run over, to whom are we giving the overflow? The blessings of the Lord are not to be hoarded, but to be generously and abundantly shared with others. Meyer concludes by exhorting us to take our cups and drink with gratitude. "Some appear to think that God does not mean them to be thoroughly happy; and if they drink their cups of joy, it must be on the sly or with words of apology. Some drink only half; or if they drink at all, they instill some bitter ingredient of their own, lest the draught should be too delicious. How often we forget that God has given us all things richly to enjoy" (1 Timothy 6:17).

Thanksgiving is the only appropriate response to Christ who was born to make all things new. Think of the psalm's ecstatic benediction, "My cup runneth over. Surely goodness and mercy shall follow me all the days of my life: and I will dwell in the house of the Lord for ever" (Psalm 23:5–6 KJV).

This chapter taken from Moody *Magazine, January/February 1998*

The Westminster Shorter Catechism is correct when it concludes that "man's chief end is to glorify God and enjoy Him forever." Why, then, are we so consumed with glorifying ourselves and seeking enjoyment for ourselves apart from Him? Perhaps this is the reason we often find life so disappointing, disruptive, and ultimately, full of regret.

We are built for significance. Our problem is not that we search for it, but that we search for it in all the wrong places.

◈

Barbara, a college sophomore who began her summer with great expectations, landed a good job in a nearby nursing home. But her summer turned into a nightmare. Before it ended Barbara was sexually assaulted by two men on the job. Deciding to drop charges due to the complicated and embarrassing legal process, Barbara found support and strength from her parents and church family.

In particular, three young men in the church sought her out to encourage and help her through the trauma. Each asked her out for an evening of fun to get away from it all. But before the evenings were over, each had asked her for sexual favors.

Struggling with a sense of deep disappointment and confusion, Barbara felt that her worth and value had been trampled. Why, she wondered, did men seem so free to use and abuse her, seeing her only as an object of their gratification? The answer came, and her liberation began, in her next semester at college as Barbara realized that she was being driven by a desire to find her sense of significance in having attention from men.

If men were attracted to and interested in her, she sensed her worth. She felt like she counted for something. Her obsession with significance had caused Barbara to order her whole life, from the clothes she wore to what she said and did, around one goal: to gain the attention of men through her sexuality. She never wanted to be provocative and did not try intentionally to be seductive. But in her dress and her words she sent all the wrong signals. Men thought she wanted sex when she was really seeking personal significance. The irony is that these relationships with men always "went south" for Barbara, finding their way to the dead-end streets of shame, loss, and confusion. No wonder despair had anchored itself in her soul.

But after years of carrying the weight of guilt and seeking deliverance from her struggle through repeated prayer and confession, Barbara found liberation in a fundamental truth: significance is secured not through our efforts or by the attention and affirmation of others; rather, her significance had already been established in the completed work of Christ for her on the cross. Armed with that reality, Barbara was set free from her burden of guilt and wrong relationships and set on the road to healthy relationships with the men in her life.

We may not be trapped in the same depths Barbara was. But we shouldn't congratulate ourselves: each of us, as we search for significance, will find other minefields waiting.

I recall being with a friend of mine, an effective teacher of God's Word, who had just returned from a week of ministry at a national conference in Canada. He was telling me how wonderful it had been to be the teacher in the Bible Hour every morning. He was obviously captured by the privilege and also thrilled with the attendees' enthusiastic response to the teaching of the Word. What he didn't know was that the year before I had been the Bible Hour teacher at that same conference. I had enjoyed the same sense of privilege he was basking in.

Do you think I could be content to encourage him and rejoice with him? I'm embarrassed to say no. I kept waiting for him to take a breath, to reach a paragraph break so that I could jump in and tell that I knew exactly how he felt. And sure enough, at the first verbal pause I was into the conversation, building a monument to me. But I walked away from that conversation asking myself, *Why do I feel so compelled to magnify me?*

I felt a loss of dignity and a sense of shame—and that surprised me. I had sought to strengthen and elevate myself; instead I felt weak and small. I had assumed that if I could enhance myself, I would feel better about myself.

More recently, I was sitting on the platform before 1,200 pastors on the opening night of a recent Pastors' Conference at Moody Bible Institute. The keynote speaker began his talk by saying, "When Tim asked me to come and speak at this year's conference ... " Immediately I thought about his statement. Tim is my associate, and we work hard to get the finest speakers possible. Often we're able to bring in high-profile Christian leaders.

I'm sorry to admit, though, that for a fleeting moment a thought resided in my mind and heart that I wish had never come: *Wait a minute. Tim didn't ask him, I did. I wonder if these pastors know that I am the one who chooses the speakers for this conference.* Thankfully, the thought didn't stay long before it was chased off by the more rational one: *What difference does it really make who chooses the speakers?* Yet that fleeting moment showed me how deeply entrenched this issue of significance is, and how readily we view most of the moments of our lives through its distorted lens.

None of us is exempt from this significance pursuit, to the point where the pursuit often becomes a significance obsession. Our problem is that we look for significance in all the wrong places. We pursue prosperity, power, position, belonging, identity, and affirmation in hopes of finally securing a sense of value and worth.

To make matters worse, this pursuit is complicated by three basic drives: pleasure, pride, and passion. Though not wrong in themselves—they are, after all, given by God—pleasure, pride, and passion turned inward in a search for significance in our own achievements and the commendation of others put us at great peril.

Unless we find our significance in God and His Son, Jesus Christ, we will experience measures of regret instead of the contentment and security that God intends for us.

❧

A pastor's wife who had served with her husband for years came to me after a recent service with tear-filled eyes, saying that she had never realized before how her obsession with significance had created such a bitter and angry spirit toward the people she and her husband served. They did their best to serve the congregation's needs, often denying themselves evenings at home, a social life, leisure, even sleep. For the most part, however, their efforts went unrecognized.

In fact, as is true in all public service, they got mostly criticism and complaints. This woman had counted on finding her sense of significance through her and her husband's efforts, and the congregation's grateful and well-deserved applause. Feeling unloved and unappreciated, her sense of significance trampled, she found anger and bitterness poisoning her heart toward the ministry God had called them to. She was disappointed, her part in the ministry disrupted, and her heart disengaged from God and the people.

But the tears in her eyes were tears of repentance and liberation as she came to realize that the congregation was not the source of her significance. "You're right, I am complete in Christ. His affirmation for faithfulness and effective service is the only thing that really matters. He's the true source of value and worth." This discovery transformed the focus of her life, leaving her free to love and serve regardless of the people's response.

All of us are driven by the compelling need to believe that we are significant. I have yet to meet the person who says, "Significance? I couldn't care less. All I want to do is fill space on this planet." Everyone wants to count for something. As author and theologian R. C. Sproul says, "We yearn to believe that in some way we are important. This inner drive is as intense as our need for water and oxygen."[1]

In fact, because our need for significance is so primary, it can easily become an obsession. Modern counseling and psychology have focused a lot of attention on obsessive behaviors, whether it's an obsession with food, tobacco, alcohol, pornography, drugs, power, work—or even an obsession with being abused! But I don't know that I've ever seen a list of obsessive behaviors that includes an addiction to the maintenance, advancement, enlargement, and protection of our significance. Yet for many of us, that is our less-than-magnificent obsession. Just as obsession with food leads to gluttony and an obsession with safety leads to anxiety and even neuroses, an obsession with our significance leads to a life of selfishness.

In psychologist Abraham Maslow's classic study of fundamental human needs, only food and safety rank as more compelling drives than significance. These intrinsic needs manage and manipulate who we are and what we do. Just as hunger drives us to find and consume food to survive, and just as we instinctively defend ourselves when we feel threatened, so we are driven as well to discover, establish, maintain, protect, and enhance our sense of significance.

Feeling significant comes as we believe we have worth, value, and dignity. Significance is knowing that our existence has made a difference after all. It doesn't have to be a great difference, just a difference. Significance is what makes a pat on the back so important. It's why affirmation is so vital. We believe we count when someone says we count. Having value and dignity are important, but depending how we seek them, we can be deluded and consumed by the search. Without a tried and proven strategy, our search for significance is a risky and treacherous adventure.

The search is risky because we live in a world full of other significance seekers who either carelessly or purposely are willing to damage our sense of worth to establish theirs. These people are often fierce competitors who get their significance through the exercise of power and control, who attempt to build the illusion that they are so significant that others will submit to their pleasure and agenda.

These significance seekers attempt to overpower us personally, relationally, sexually, socially, and athletically, and in the process they may very well destroy our sense of worth. Complicating the scene are those of us who find our sense of significance in the attention of these power brokers and as a result become their easy prey. There is not a realm of life that isn't damaged, sometimes fatally and irretrievably, by the significance seekers of the worlds in which we live.

Yet the problem does not really begin with others pursuing their significance to our detriment. It begins with the self-inflicted damage we cause in our own significance pursuit. Our obsession with our own significance is such an insatiable hunger that its impact is felt in every area of life, creating realms of regret that put our sense of worth in peril.

⸙

This striving to advance our own significance shows up typically when we're driving in traffic. Getting cut off, not being allowed to merge into a lane, or worse yet, getting ticketed for an offense, are all affronts to our sense of significance. As Christians, we may not have enough words and gestures to express how we really feel at moments like that, so we resort to intense stares, muttering under our breath in the hope that the other driver can read lips.

Or we aggressively retaliate. I have had more than one "out of body" experience on the highway after I blew an anger fuse. Hovering over myself I watched in amazement: "Was that really you, Stowell? I had no idea you were like that." Immediately I feel a sense of loss and shame after exalting and defending myself on the interstate.

This obsession with significance is why we are so defensive when someone seeks to "improve" us through criticism. You'd think we would thank those whom God sends to help knock off our rough edges, but instead we resist their input and intimidate our advisors to protect our sense of significance that has been threatened by criticism.

This obsession is also why some of us are embittered by unchangeable personal realities like our size, shape, color of skin, or physical deformity. Society establishes acceptable norms for our looks and style. When for His good purposes God creates in us some deviation from society's norms, it is easy for us to feel less than significant and culturally unacceptable. This leads to an insecure spirit that damages our capacity to find fulfillment and satisfaction in God's purposes for us.

Similarly, men and women who are disappointed in courtship and remain single can be vulnerable. They may be left with a deep sense of rejection and a haunting feeling of insignificance that makes it hard for them to have any positive relationships with members of the opposite sex.

Our compulsion for significance makes us vulnerable to a legion of verbal sins, including gossip, slander, boasting, lying, immoral chatter, and other unkind blows by our tongues. In all this our character, our personhood, is eroded. The significance addiction leaves us vulnerable to a host of other personal failures that complicate life and debilitate us spiritually and socially. It may surprise you to learn that many people have affairs not because they are drooling with uncontrolled passion, but because for the first time in their lives someone has come along and made them feel significant during a time when they especially needed it.

We are quick to violate basic principles of stewardship and burden ourselves with debt to accumulate things that enhance our significance on the social scene. And to advance our significance in the marketplace, we may violate our integrity as we exchange conscience and commitment to Christ for a significant title on our business card.

Significance seekers are unable to serve others unless there is an advantage to be gained, unable to sacrifice to advance a cause that is not their own, unwilling to suffer if necessary for another's sake, and unable to surrender to any agenda—corporate, family, or church—that impedes the progress of their pursuit of significance. This obsession renders us useless in terms of making constructive contributions to our families, friends, society, and churches. And even when managed to magnificent outward success, the significance obsession ultimately brings loss, shame, guilt, emptiness, and regret.

◦❧

Because our personhood affects every relationship we have, few obsessions are more devastating than seeking to satisfy this primal need at the expense of others. Families are victimized by husbands and fathers whose significance is established only when they are in absolute, unchallenged control. Crossing a significance seeker who is the head of the home—a father or single parent—can lead to anger, violence, and other forms of intimidation and manipulation. Significance seekers who head homes like this never say they are wrong or sorry.

We fathers too often are willing to absent ourselves from home as we seek to establish our significance in a place where we feel more capable of accomplishment—the office or even the golf course. We look for compliments and job advancement not to provide for our families but to feed our egos.

Meanwhile, mothers at home may feel that because motherhood is an undervalued profession they are less significant than they want to be. Sometimes a mother or father, in the name of finding significance, locates a "significant other" and quits the marriage emotionally and then physically, leaving children and spouse to fend for themselves. At other times, workaholic parents neglect time with children, supposing that significance is found in performance. Some parents communicate that a child's significance is measured not in his parents' unconditional love and acceptance, but rather in performing up to their expectations. In these and other ways our misunderstanding of true significance places our families at risk.

Similarly, our significance search affects our friendships. Often we forge friendships simply because we draw significance from associating with the other person. But this only leads to an overpossessiveness and unwarranted jealousy on the part of the significance seeker, which in turn leads to friction and the death of the friendship. Many couples violate basic moral principles in their courtship for fear of losing this person who offers so much significance now and the prospect of future significance in marriage.

Interestingly, our students who work with gangs here in Chicago attest to the fact that very few if any young people join gangs for violence, sex, drugs, and crime. They join because the gang is the only place where they find acceptance and personal significance. This addiction to significance helps explain why our kids choose friends we don't approve of, and why a well-educated, decent girl gets hooked up with a guy who has nothing to offer but trouble and hurt. That's just the point. He needs her, and that makes her feel significant, accepted, and affirmed. This addiction is why we refuse to forgive and even seek revenge against those who have hurt us.

✸

Not only does a significance addict damage his personhood, bringing loss and regret to himself and his relationships, but many of society's problems reflect the same pattern. Some cultural structures enhance the significance of one race or gender or class over another. Those caught in the lower levels of the system feel a loss of significance, while those in power don't wish to share their significance with others. Thus people march, riot, and even start wars. The poor, the disabled, and the immigrants who feel they are ignored rise up to demand their place and their worth. Some politicians, seemingly caring for others' needs, stand with the underclass with a desire only to inflate their own significance rather than to benefit those they stand with. Homosexuals, people of color, the poor, and women take to the streets to demand a significant place in society.

Such highly dangerous pursuits as rape, abuse, violence, drugs, and crime often are the sad outcomes of a desperate search for significance in a dramatically depersonalized society. Even abortion is an outcome of the search for significance. If an unborn child threatens a mother's agenda for significance, society argues that the child is expendable.

Much of the despair and regret in the world around us can be attributed to our inability to understand and remedy this obsession for significance at any cost. And instead of helping us, society's power structures relentlessly fan the flame.

The constant refrain we hear is that those who are perceived as significant have arrived and are models of the ultimate pursuit of life. In our culture, significance is measured less by the contributions we make to society than by our power, performance, position, and prosperity.

Look at the world of college and professional sports. The message is clear: winners are the only ones who count. There's little applause for finishing second. Character doesn't win pennants. As the late baseball manager Leo Durocher once said, "Nice guys finish last." Even more debilitating, our society cares little about the integrity or character of significant people or how they become significant. The point is to attain and maintain your significance. The process is irrelevant. Television talk shows specialize in staging and interviewing American's "significant" ones. I'm still waiting for David Letterman or Jay Leno to say, "Now I know you're significant, but what we all want to know is whether you have maintained personal integrity as you've achieved your significance." Madonna would have a hard time fielding that question. So would the executives at Enron.

In a sense, ours is a "Little Jack Horner" world where the game of significance ignores the deeper issues of right and wrong. In a moment of what for him was stellar significance, Jack stuck his thumb into a Christmas pie, pulled out a plum, raised it high in the air, and proclaimed, "What a good boy am I." Pleased with his performance, he went public and sought significance through the applause and affirmation of those around him.

It's this Little Jack Horner syndrome that makes us willing to do whatever is necessary to become significant. But if we ignore the process, we unwittingly erode our sense of worth by clouding our conscience. Regardless of the pinnacle we reach, our significance quest finally becomes hollow.

Jesus once described a significantly prosperous, powerful, and well-positioned man who had so much that he built new barns to hold it all. This highly significant person smugly said to himself, "Eat, drink and be merry." Jesus said God's reply to the man was, "You fool! This very night your life will be demanded from you. Then who will get what you have prepared for yourself?" (Luke 12:19–20 NIV). This is the ultimate regret, the regret of eternal loss.

Most important, however, our obsession with significance creates another realm of regret that strikes destructive blows to the cause of Christ. Bringing our uncured addiction into the church damages the reputation of Christ, the enhancement of His glory, and the advance of His cause.

There are pastors who use the church as a platform to launch a personal significance campaign. They do battle with deacons, elders, and charter members who also want to use the church to enhance their power and position. The division and disruption that come as a result of these battles stain the reputation of Christ in the community. Added to this is the competition between churches to be the biggest and the best, discouraging faithful smaller works and swelling with pride those who are blessed with more.

There are also those who proclaim that you can satisfy your longing for significance not in Christ and Him alone, but by coercing Him through "faith" to make you happy, healthy, and prosperous. There are televangelists who have preyed on the uninformed by appealing to their need for significance, making these people feel significant if they send money, which in turn enhances the significance of the charlatan preacher.

Still others have dishonored the name of Christ by allowing their significance in His work to delude them into believing that they were above obedience when it came to money, women, or power. They have publicly taken the name of Christ through the trough of disgrace.

This obsessive pursuit obstructs authentic Christian living. Our obsession with significance stimulates things that are counter to the values and behavior of those who follow Christ. Authentic Christianity does not call for defensive responses, but a vulnerable spirit that we might be taught by the Spirit. Jesus calls us to have a meek and humble heart, like Him (Matthew 11:29). True Christianity calls us to complement one another, not to compete. It holds us accountable to be people of unflinching integrity and to care more about the kingdom of God and eternity than about material things, regardless of how significant they may make us feel here.

A proper understanding of our walk with Christ plants our security firmly on our unshakable relationship with Him. It speaks against connecting our security to persons or possessions, which only exposes us to the fear of rejection and loss. Christians are not to live to please others or their culture, but rather to please God. The jealousy, greed, possessiveness, and manipulative behavior that characterize significance seekers are inconsistent with faith in Christ. Authentic Christians continue to do well regardless of whether they are recognized or affirmed.

As those who imitate Christ, we don't focus on our rights and privileges, but are willing to sacrifice them for greater gain in His work. We are shaken, but not fatally so, even by significant loss, because we can't lose that which is ultimately significant to us. Gossip, slander, and bragging become unnecessary for those who are growing in Christ. We are to focus on encouraging, helping, and affirming others.

Christ calls us to rejoice with those who rejoice, which frees us to feel good about those who accomplish great things instead of feeling jealous and seeking to bring others down. Following Christ means that we are in control of our priorities and reject the impulse to be either workaholics or "leisureholics" when it comes to life's important responsibilities.

What is the underlying reason we as Christians often feel a sense of failure as we attempt to accomplish those things we know God wants us to do? The answer may be found at the feet of our addiction to the enlargement, advancement, and defense of our own significance.

The debilitating effects of the Christian's self-centered quest for significance goes beyond the personal to the church at large. Even a casual analysis of American culture reveals that over the last few decades we have turned a dramatic corner. Americans are no longer culturally committed to the Judeo-Christian principles that have undergirded our law and society from the beginning. Americans have now moved into a neo-pagan environment where the values that Christians hold to be nonnegotiable are no longer politically correct. In fact, they are culturally unacceptable.

In a very real sense, we Christians are becoming more and more of an underclass in this society. Our convictions are at best discounted and at worst mocked by the prevalent philosophies promoted by the media and other significant influences. We are increasingly viewed as less-significant people in our culture. Think what this means if we are obsessed with significance in the eyes of our pagan culture. Our seeking after cultural standing could very well undermine the strength of our faith, and weaken our commitment to stand with courage in the face of subtle opposition and perhaps even open persecution. The history of the church is littered with individual Christians and institutions that sought to remain culturally significant and in the process eroded their commitment and distinctiveness in Christ.

Maintaining a thoughtful, balanced, and just posture within a pagan culture is a worthy goal. But there comes a time when standing for that which is true may invite rejection by a culture whose values are so dramatically opposed to the values of God's kingdom.

We must keep in mind that the early church advanced the cause of Christ in a culture that viewed Christians not just as irrelevant, but as enemies of the Empire. If you named the name of Christ in that day, you lost your cultural significance. You could also wind up as lunch for the lions in the Roman arenas as the crowds roared with excitement.

The early church didn't seek its significance in acceptance and affirmation by the pagan world. It had found its significance in Christ. Their liberation from this obsession gave these believers the capacity to be courageous. As a result, they glorified the significance of His name and advanced His cause in such a compelling way that Christianity ultimately became the official Roman state religion some three hundred years after the death of Christ.

We make a difference when our uniqueness is clothed in the grace and truth of Jesus Christ, not when we capitulate in order to become credible in a pagan society. Great schools have become thoroughly secularized because the faculty and administration desired to be credible and significant in the educational world at the expense of truth, heritage, and their mission. Entire denominations, great movements, churches, and causes throughout history have been derailed because the urge for cultural significance led to compromise in their methods and their message. Their quest for society's approval had more force than truth and a solid commitment to be significant in God's eyes at any cost.

~&

The greatest danger of our obsession with significance, however, is measured in its crippling effect on our ability to fulfill God's purpose for us—to display His glory to others. Even if our significance obsession would not threaten our personhood, family relationships, authentic Christianity or even an impact on society at large, this peril alone warrants our concern. Scripture affirms that redemption was accomplished in us for the express purpose of releasing us to enhance His glory and advance His cause. (See 1 Corinthians 6:19–20 and Ephesians 1:6, 11–14.)

God's glory through us is the visible expression of His marvelous character in our lives. We display God's glory by replicating all that He is. In the process, we declare His significance and worth by giving Him credit for all that we are and all that we do. In Philippians 1:20 Paul declared: "I eagerly expect and hope that I will in no way be ashamed, but will have sufficient courage so that now as always Christ will be exalted in my body, whether by life or by death" (NIV).

If we are obsessed with exalting our own significance, we are unable to exalt His significance. The two are mutually exclusive endeavors. You can't have it both ways. Paul said in the next verse "For to me, to live is Christ and to die is gain" (NIV). If our formula is "For me to live is personal gain and to die is Christ," then we forfeit the essential element of what it means to glorify Christ and His kingdom. And if we spend our lives seeking to enhance our significance by acquiring position, power, prosperity, and other cultural status symbols, we disable our capacity for deeds that advance and enhance the kingdom of Christ. To disciples who were worried about this kind of significance Christ admonished, "Seek first his kingdom." Until we are liberated from this obsession, we will not be free to glorify God by expressing His significance and doing significant things for His eternal kingdom. And those two objectives are God's primary reason for redeeming and placing us on the planet.

Michelangelo is said to have often painted with a brush in one hand and a shielded candle in the other to prevent his shadow from covering the masterpiece he was creating. As God works through us to craft His glory and gain, we must be careful that our shadows are not cast across the canvas of His work.

Christ and Christ alone is preeminent. He needs no competition. He is the only truly significant person in the universe. He deserves our commitment to reflect His significance, not our own. In Colossians 1:13–18 Paul catalogued the ultimate, unsurpassed significance of Christ:

> For [God] has rescued us from the dominion of darkness and brought us into the kingdom of the Son he loves, in whom we have redemption, the forgiveness of sins. He is the image of the invisible God, the firstborn over all creation. For by him all things were created: things in heaven and on earth, visible and invisible, whether thrones or powers or rulers or authorities; all things were created by him and for him. He is before all things, and in him all things hold together. And he is the head of the body, the church; he is the beginning and the firstborn from among the dead. (NIV)

Paul concluded with this affirmation: "So that in everything he might have the supremacy." *He.* Not us!

This chapter taken from Perilous Pursuits, *Moody Publishers, 1994*

C an pride be redeemed and made to work for God's glory? Despite all the evidence around us, God's Word says that it can. The good news is that the solution to unredeemed pride is not suppression or eradication. Like our pleasure and passion instincts, pride is part of our created makeup.

Bringing the "pride platoon" over to our side of the field is a matter of getting God's perspective on pride and understanding His intended purpose for its proper expression.

The pride platoon loves to wreak havoc on us. What can we do, then, with this force that resides so powerfully in our hearts? Our first impulse is to try and eradicate it. We reason that we can kill pride through some act of our will. After a strong sermon on pride, we awake Monday morning resolving to renounce pride, to delete it from our agendas. "I will live today without pride," we declare. Others wake up and say, "I will adopt in its place the quality of humility," which we rightly assume is the other side of pride. But we soon find that the struggle remains.

The reality is that no one can escape pride. As usual, C. S. Lewis described pride as well as anybody:

> There is one vice of which no man in the world is free; which every one in the world loathes when he sees it in someone else; and of which hardly any people, except Christians, ever imagine that they are guilty of them-selves...The essential vice, the utmost evil, is Pride. Unchastity, anger, greed, drunkenness, and all that, are mere fleabites in comparison: it was through Pride that the devil became the devil: Pride leads to every other vice: it is the complete anti-God state of mind. [1]

Since pride is "the essential vice," some seek to express humility by being quiet, not smiling much, and certainly not laughing loudly. We impose on our spirit a mellowness; with great tenderness we try to be sure that we put everyone else far out in front of us, and never once do we value who we are. This is humility, we tell ourselves. We try to talk slowly and carefully, never raising our voices in excitement and certainly never expressing any point of view that may be important to us, particularly if the issue is controversial. And most important, we lace our sentences with spiritual talk at every opportunity. Many of us assume the posture of doormats, and as we respond weakly and solemnly, we welcome foot traffic to walk across our lives. I suspect that most people would say, "If this is what it takes to defeat pride and convert it to the right side of my life, if this is humility, I think I'll pass on this spiritual pro-ject, have one less reward, and go on to a different spiritual challenge."

But I have good news. That kind of humility is not what God demands. In fact, His Word never tells us to eradicate pride and assume a wimpish demeanor. Pride is an expression of something that has been created deep in our souls to give us the power and capacity to honor and advance God's king-dom.

⤸

Pride is that part of ourselves that we call ego. Men take a particularly bad rap in this area, but I don't know a woman who would want to have a man with no ego either as a friend or a life partner. Most women are not enthralled with passive manhood. The issue for all of us, men and women, is whether our egos are Spirit directed. If our egos with their determination, energy, and power are directed by God's Spirit—so that we are energetic, enthusiastic, and insistent about God's glory and gain—we've got a powerful force for good. At that point, the pride platoon has come over on our side of the line and is playing ball with us for God's glory.

So the issue is not pride eradicated, but pride revised. Our pride must be refocused to honor Him. True humility is a life that has put pride in its place.

Pride has many self-focused manifestations that are always out of bounds: arrogance, insolence, violence, boasting, and other forms of self-elevation. Scripture, however, describes certain aspects of pride in positive ways. When this energy within is refocused on the magnificence of God, instead of the magnificent me, we are compelled to praise and serve our marvelous Maker.

The prophet Jeremiah said:

This is what the LORD says: "Let not the wise man boast of his wisdom or the strong man boast of his strength or the rich man boast of his riches, but let him who boasts boast about this: that he understands and knows me, that I am the LORD, who exercises kindness, justice and righteousness on earth, for in these I delight," declares the LORD. *9:23–24 (NIV)*

Jeremiah understood this redemptive refocus. Notice that the one who called for boasting here was God Himself. But it is pride that's properly placed, not in ourselves but in Him who deserves our attention and affirmation.

In the intriguing French film entitled *My Father's Glory,* a husband and wife living in Paris take a vacation in the countryside with their two boys and the boys' aunt and uncle. Upon arrival, it becomes apparent that Marcel, the older boy, deeply admires his dad. He is embarrassed that his uncle dominates and intimidates his father. Early one morning, the two men go hunting. Marcel begs to go with them and although his father seems to be weakening, his uncle firmly says that this is not something for a boy to be doing. As the men leave, Marcel sneaks off and follows them for a distance.

As the hunters walk through the valley chatting and looking for quail, he walks along the ridge, hiding behind bushes when he thinks they might see him. Quite by accident, Marcel flushes two royal partridges out of the bush. As they rise, his father spots them and raises his gun, as does his uncle. But Marcel's father is faster, and fires twice. Both birds come plummeting to the ground at Marcel's feet.

Ecstatic at his father's triumph, Marcel grabs the quail and lifts them high, one in each hand, and his shouts echo through the hills: "He killed them, both of them. He did it!" As the camera zooms away from the boy, the gorgeous beauty of the hills and valley envelops him as he stands, arms lifted with quail in hand, raising his father's glory to the sky.

It is that kind of redeemed pride that marks authentic believers. No longer consumed with ourselves, we realize that we belong to the Creator, and as we behold the marvel of His works and wisdom we find our hearts swelling with pride that He is our Father and we are His children. We lift our voices instinctively in worship and praise to His unsurpassed glory. Such pride is not arrogant, insolent, or self-absorbed. It is the energy within stirred by the greatness of our God. It is the energy that catapults us to glorify God.

Whether we're like Marcel, who refused to take credit for kicking up the quail but rather consumed himself with his father's glory, shouting his father's praise for all to hear, or like my Hebrew professor who told the bank teller that

134

it wasn't that he was an honest man but that Christ had changed his life. Praise is the natural response to pride focused away from self and to God where it rightly belongs. No wonder Scripture says, "Through Jesus, therefore, let us continually offer to God a sacrifice of praise—the fruit of lips that confess his name . . . for with such sacrifices God is pleased" (Hebrews 13:15–16 NIV).

This chapter taken from Perilous Pursuits, *Moody Publishers, 1994*

T he little village was so small and remote that we were the first foreign visitors to come there in thirty-eight years. We sat in a simple little home some sixty miles from Minsk, Belarus, with one of the students who had come to MBI from the former Soviet Union, his mother, and his pastor. I listened to Pastor Ivan tell of his work in that area and watched the movements of his battle-lined face. I was unprepared for the story he told, but I will never forget its impact on my life. Here was an unsung hero who has been faithful through many years of oppression and difficulty.

During the severe oppression of Russian believers under Stalin, this pastor, then a young man, was asked by the Soviet secret police, the KGB, to report on the affairs of the congregation to the secret police while still serving as pastor. The state would take good care of him, and no one would know. As I listened to Ivan, I wondered what I might have done had I been in his shoes. This was an opportunity for safety and security for this pastor and his family, and also an opportunity to share in the significance of being a part of one of the world's most powerful forces.

Obviously, though, Ivan was a man who had long before found his significance in Christ. He was free to look those KGB agents in the eye and say no. "No, I cannot do that to my Lord or my people." He knew that his refusal to betray Christ for a ticket to his own significance would probably earn him arrest and a ticket to a Siberian labor camp. And that's exactly what happened. Put on a ship with fifteen hundred other prisoners, he was off to Siberia on a journey during which six hundred prisoners died in a boiler explosion on the ship. He was force marched across the frozen, windswept Siberian tundra to the prison camp where he arrived with most of his shoe leather worn away from the forced march. He served there for ten years.

"Were there any other Christians in your camp?" I asked, and the interpreter translated.

"Yes. We would get together often to read the Word to one another, encourage one another, and sing hymns of praise to God. During the last few years of our imprisonment, we were sent out in a sixty-mile radius from their camp to help build towns in the Siberian wilderness for Stalin.

"As we went to these remote places, the Christians would gather in fellowship. Often we were able to share our faith quietly with the people in the villages." He paused, with an obvious sense of satisfaction and joy on his face, then added, "You know, today there are literally hundreds of churches all over Siberia as a result of those fellowship groups of Christians during those ruthless years of the oppression."

I listened to this remarkable story, marveling at the power of God that can take a person committed to the glory of Christ and the gain of His kingdom, and use him so dramatically for the advance of the gospel. It was as though God, in His desire to establish outposts in the Siberian wilderness, said to Stalin, the dictator who railed against God, "Take some of My finest servants, those who are not addicted to their significance but to My work, and send them as missionaries to Siberia. And you pay the bill!" And so some of God's finest were sent off, not knowing why they went, but simply being faithful to God.

Being free from our obsession to our own significance releases us to follow a fourfold pattern of commitment that makes us wonderfully usable in the Lord's hands. Through this pattern God has used parents, janitors, presidents, and kings to bring glory to His name and accomplish great things for Himself. In fact, it is the very pattern that Christ followed when He accomplished our redemption, the greatest gain for God's glory and plan that has ever been accomplished. This is the commitment of those who want to take the initiative and position themselves to be used by God.

Here are the four essential commitments that Christ lived out in His earthly ministry and His death on the cross to purchase our redemption. He was willing to surrender to the Father's will, willing to sacrifice His privileges and position, willing to serve, and willing to suffer.

Without those four essential commitments, Christ could not have taken the initiative to accomplish the great work of redemption and secure its benefits for us: hell canceled, heaven guaranteed, and the redeemed being made fully significant in the Father, free to advance and enhance God's glory through Christ's power in us.

The commitments are most fully described in Philippians 2. Verses 3–4 (NIV) help to set the context for us, a fascinating one in which we are exhorted to abandon our addiction to our significance: "Do nothing out of selfish ambition or vain conceit, but in humility consider others better than yourselves. Each of you should look not only to your own interests, but also to the interests of others."

It is important to note how absolute the exhortation is. We are to do nothing out of self-advancing motives. Nor are we to focus only on those things that benefit us. I think it would be interesting if, for one day, we kept track of the number of times we were either tempted to—or succumbed to the temptation to—do, say, or think something that deliberately served our significance only.

We would probably be shocked at how full the page would be. There would be entries noting the times we jumped into a conversation to look or sound important and intelligent, or just to elbow our way into the discussion. Other entries would record the times we said no to someone else's need because it conflicted with our need; the times we bent truth to protect or enlarge our significance in other people's eyes. There might be an entry or two noting our resentment at someone who achieved a higher level of significance than we did, or how we let our thoughts spill out in gossip or slander. I could go on, but you get the idea.

In sharp contrast, Paul calls on us to adopt the mind of Christ. Instead of being consumed with ourselves (Philippians 2:3–4), we should, "Let this mind be in you, which was also in Christ Jesus" (v. 5, KJV). Then in verses 6–8 (NIV) we come to the fourfold mindset that Christ committed Himself to in order to accomplish His Father's glory and plan for His life:

> Who, being in very nature God, did not consider equality with God something to be grasped, but made himself nothing, taking the very nature of a servant, being made in human likeness. And being found in appearance as a man, he humbled himself and became obedient to death—even death on a cross!

What better way to display our liberation from an obsession with our own significance than to pattern our lives after Jesus Christ, who is far and away the most significant One in the universe (Colossians 1:14–18). If Christ, who had every right to celebrate and advance His significance, could take the initiative to accomplish His Father's glory by submitting Himself to this vital fourfold process, then the implications for us are profound. How can we, who have no intrinsic significance in comparison to Christ, refuse to serve our Father's glory and His gain by seeking to advance and enhance ourselves? We can't! That's why the authentic, liberated follower of God adopts the pattern of Christ. Let's look at the first two components of this fourfold commitment.

Step One: Surrender

Step one in taking the initiative to fulfill our redemptive calling is a willingness to surrender to an agenda bigger than ourselves—to God's agenda. Philippians 2:6–8 make it clear that Christ was willing to get beyond the power, privileges, and perks of His supreme position in the universe and commit Himself to His Father's gain and glory.

Surrendering to God's agenda in and through us requires a clear view of the agendas we have prescribed for ourselves. Most people's lists of things they consider important would include personal peace, happiness, comfort, prosperity, security, friends, good health, fulfilling experiences, and reaching their full potential.

The above list should make the need for our surrender obvious, for those plans often conflict or ignore God's plan for us. It's true that God may and often does provide for us measures of peace, prosperity, position, fulfillment, and other things on our lists, but our surrender to God's plan is a statement that we will not live for these things. They are not the things that drive us, but are simply side benefits that come through the sovereign pleasure of God.

Let's never forget the great benefit to God's glory and kingdom that has come through the lives of thousands of people who have surrendered to agendas beyond their own. Some have gone to faraway lands as missionaries. Mothers have surrendered careers and opportunities for significance to teach their children God's truth. Fathers have changed careers or turned down promotions that conflicted with God's will for them or their families. Pastors have faithfully served in out-of-the-way places where no one knows their names or asks them to speak at high-profile conferences.

Surrendering to something greater than ourselves reminds me of the time that D.L. Moody first heard the rich, full voice of Ira Sankey at a Sunday school convention. In his trademark direct way, Mr. Moody went to Sankey and said, "I have been looking for someone like you for years. You must leave your position at once and join me in my work in Chicago."

Sankey protested that he already had a job in Cincinnati, but it was to no avail; Moody persisted, and Sankey finally realized he had to surrender to a plan greater than his own. He joined Moody in Chicago, and the pair became the greatest evangelistic team of the nineteenth century.

Earlier in this century, a young Bible college graduate responded similarly to the call of God. He intended to start a church in the Upper Peninsula of Michigan where, in those days, the logging camps were brutal places to live and work. Going into one of the camps, he tried to start by inviting the children of the town to Sunday school. He went door-to-door in the toughest part of town, where even the police refused to patrol, looking for children for his Sunday school. Most of those doors were slammed in his face, but two boys, Les and Jay, asked their mothers if they could go. Week after week, year after year, that pastor drove into the tough part of town and picked up those boys for Sunday school.

Les and Jay eventually accepted Christ, were discipled under the pastor's care, and when it came time to go to college they too, like their pastor, went to Bible school to train for ministry. Upon graduation, Jay Walsh sensed God's call to become a missionary in Bangladesh, a land where very few missionaries had gone. Jay forged a ministry in Bangladesh that established a base for the effective spread of the gospel.

Meanwhile, back in the States, an agnostic doctor was led to the Lord and dedicated the rest of his life to medical service for Christ. He wanted to use his skills to serve in a place where there was little medical help and great need for the gospel. So Dr. Viggo Olson found himself on his way to Bangladesh, following in the steps of Jay Walsh. While there, Dr. Olson wrote the story of his conversion and surrender to missionary service that became the best-selling book, *Daktar*. Many doctors were influenced for Christ through the book, and hundreds of young people, after reading it and hearing Dr. Olson's testimony, gave their lives to the cause of world missions.

Les Ollillia, the other boy from that Michigan logging town, became a young evangelist. Les moved to the Midwest, presenting the gospel to young people until God tapped him on the shoulder to become the president of Northland Bible College in Wisconsin, where he is multiplying his surrendered spirit in the lives of many young people who will replicate his commitment around the world.

It's amazing what God can do through one pastor, unknown and unheralded in an obscure logging camp—and uninterested in his own significance—who surrenders himself to the glory of God and the gain of His kingdom. Your surrender may not take you into career ministry. Your calling may be in the marketplace as someone who views a career not as an opportunity to accumulate wealth, position, and power, but as an avenue whereby you can glorify Christ and advance His kingdom by your influence.

My friend Clayton Brown, founder and chief executive officer of Clayton Brown and Associates, one of the leading bond houses in Chicago, recently told me over lunch that although he could sell his business, retire, and be comfortable for the rest of his life, he wasn't ready to do that yet. Why? Because he knew that the day he sold his business, he would lose his ministry in the Chicago Loop. Clay has held weekly Bible studies in the Loop for years, and today there are businesspeople who know and live for Christ because of those studies. Young people regularly seek Clay's advice as to how one meshes business and a commitment to Christ, and he helps them. Clayton Brown is a man who has surrendered to an agenda beyond himself.

This kind of commitment has marked God's people for generations. Susannah Wesley, whose pastor-husband was busy in the ministry and not very involved at home, gave birth to nineteen children, of whom only nine lived to adulthood. She reared her children for the most part single-handedly. It was said that Susannah gathered with her children every day for two hours to read Scripture, pray with them, and teach them the things of God. Her years of faithfulness paid off when God used two of those children—John and Charles Wesley—to bring revival to the British Isles and fill our hymnals with hymns that continue to bless us to this day.

Stack up the results of lives that have been committed to God's program rather than to personal comfort and convenience, and the comparison is dramatic. If the mind of Christ is to be ours, we must gladly surrender ourselves in every area of life to His glory and gain through us. God calls us to surrender to His agenda in the arenas of our money, our motives, our time, and our attitudes. He calls us to surrender to His agenda at home and in the marketplace. There is no segment of life where surrendering self to serve His glory and gain does not apply.

Step Two: Sacrifice

Philippians 2:6–8 reveals a second commitment of Christ's that must be ours as well. It was a willingness to sacrifice in order that God's will might be accomplished through His life. What a stunning truth: even though Jesus was God, He did not cling to the privileges of His position. Instead, He willingly emptied Himself (v. 7). Although we will never understand fully all that this tremendous sacrifice meant for Christ, we can see several levels at which He emptied Himself to come and redeem us.

The first level of sacrifice was that of His privileges and rights as the God of the universe. Emptying Himself meant that Christ had to give up the voluntary use of many of His attributes. For instance, He yielded His omnipresence to be confined in the body of a baby, and His omnipotence to endure the cross without overpowering His enemies with ten thousand angels. Christ also sacrificed the "perks of paradise"—the glory, praise, and honor bestowed upon Him by the angelic hosts, all the splendor of what it meant to be Creator, Sustainer, and Ruler of the universe—to be born in a lowly stable while the world slept unaware.

Jesus even sacrificed things that ordinary humans expect to enjoy in the course of life: the reliability of intimate friendships, being understood and accepted for who He was, having a place to lay His head, and a little money in His pocket. Ultimately, Christ made the most intense sacrifice of all: giving His body to be hung on the cross like a criminal, having the sins of the entire race heaped upon Him, and dying the death of a despised outcast.

The bottom line is this: Christ voluntarily emptied Himself of anything and everything that stood in the way of the glory and gain of His Father through Him.

What about us? Although rights, privileges, pleasures, possessions, expectations, and well-formed plans may not be wrong in and of themselves, are we willing to hold them loosely and even let them go—to sacrifice them—if emptying ourselves of them will enable us to fulfill God's agenda for our lives?

I find it interesting that as we challenge this generation with the unsurpassed cause of spreading the gospel, we have no trouble exciting teens and young adults to seriously consider giving themselves to career ministry, and enlisting them for training in schools like Moody. Our problem is with parents who get their kids off to the side and caution them about going into something that is not a "solid, stable" career, who urge their children to get a "real job" and then maybe God will use them to help others do what they're contemplating doing at this point.

Surrendering to God's agenda may mean sacrificing our children—or our goods, reputation, comfort, convenience, and a whole list of other things we hold so tightly in our hands as well as those things we hope and plan for.

I think back to Jesus Christ's call to Peter, Andrew, James, and John to follow Him. To obey, they had to let go of their fishing nets. I've often wondered about the "nets" of money, people, plans, things, and comfort in our hands that inhibit us from making a full commitment to following Christ. Those things may be valuable to us. But in the light of who Jesus Christ is, they become insignificant next to His glory and eternal gain. The issue for us is whether, like the disciples, we are willing to let go of our nets for the sake of Christ's work.

Sacrificing our sense of significance to magnify Christ's significance may pose many strategic challenges. Several years ago, while our family was preparing for a vacation trip to Florida to visit grandparents, I got bad news from our mechanic. The transmission in our old car was in no shape for a drive all the way to Florida. It would have to be repaired first. That would have been fine, except that we were leaving the next day. The mechanic told me the soonest he could get the work done was the middle of the next week, effectively canceling our vacation.

As I sat at my desk mulling the disappointing news, the phone rang. It was a man in our church who had heard that we were going to Florida and was concerned about our whole family traveling in our undersized car. He had no idea of the transmission problem. "Pastor, God has been good to my wife and me, and one of our joys is to be able to share God's blessings with others. We'd like you to take one of our cars for your trip to Florida. You pick the car."

Both cars were very nice and certainly a major step up from what we had planned to drive. So I chose a car, and we happily packed our family in and left for Florida. This was one of those cars that turns heads on the highway. I have to admit that I've rarely felt so significant—in the fallen sense of the word—as when I drove that Lincoln Town Car to Florida.

On the way home, we stopped for gas at the self-serve pumps. Self-serve seemed a contradiction in terms for a car like that—I doubt that it had ever been to a self-serve pump before (this was back when gas stations actually had attendants to "fill 'er up"). As I stood there pumping the gas, I noticed a man standing by the pumps staring at the car. He walked over, looked admiringly at the car, and asked me, "How do you like your car?"

That was a tough question to field, because I didn't want to tell him that it wasn't my car. It seemed like the war raged in my soul for a long time, although it was just a few seconds. Would I be willing to sacrifice my undeserved sense of significance to magnify the integrity of Christ through my life? I knew what I had to do. "Well, it's not my car, but I like it very much."

Frankly, that wasn't much of a sacrifice compared to what we are called to sacrifice on many other occasions to magnify Christ's name and advance His cause. But for me it was a rather dramatic reminder of how tough it is at times to sacrifice our significance, which seems so compelling, and surrender to an agenda beyond ourselves.

We can step out for Christ and become participants in the glorious agenda He has for us—to glorify Him through our lives and accomplish great gain for His kingdom. Though we will sometimes struggle against relapses into our significance obsession, the liberating power of Christ enables us to embrace the commitments of surrender and sacrifice that make us greatly usable to Him.

This chapter taken from Perilous Pursuits, *Moody Publishers, 1994*

FOUR

AM I A SOLDIER OF THE CROSS?

```
┌─────────────────────────────────────┐
│                                      │
│        E I G H T E E N               │
│             ∽                        │
│         F l a v o r i n g            │
│         O u r   W o r l d            │
│         — f o r   H i m              │
│                                      │
└─────────────────────────────────────┘
```

S everal weeks after September 11, 2001, John MacArthur was invited to appear on *Larry King Live* to discuss how a loving God could permit the atrocities of 9/11. Rabbi Harold Kushner; Deepak Chopra, a spiritualist from California; and Dr. Hathout, a scholar of Islam and senior adviser to the Muslim Public Affairs Council, were also members of the panel. At one point, Larry King turned to Dr. MacArthur and asked him if he believed that Jesus is the only way to God and that those who reject Him are not going to heaven. John's answer was biblical and forthright. But in the face of Larry King's pointed questions and the inclusive perspectives of the other panelists, his views were quickly discarded.

As I watched how challenging it was for John to orally defend the fact that Jesus is the only way, I was reminded of how effectively Lisa Beamer had drawn the attention of the same interviewer to the value of Jesus just two weeks earlier. It wasn't that Dr. MacArthur bungled the opportunity. He didn't. It's just tough to "talk" the theology of Jesus into a world that despises His claims.

Whether Lisa knew it or not, she was "light" in one of the darkest seasons of grief and confusion in the history of our nation.

Her husband had become a hero of major proportions when he sacrificed his life to avert a fourth plane from victimizing another target on that crisp September morning. Left alone with two small boys and pregnant with her third child, she captured the attention of America with her unusual strength and poise in the midst of such devastating circumstances.

It was just days after 9/11 when she made her first of several appearances on *Larry King Live*. Speaking of her husband's role on that tragic day, she told Larry King,

"He called the GTE Airfone operator about 9:45 in the morning and started reporting to her what was going on in the plane, including that there were hijackers and they had taken over the cockpit and possibly killed the crew. He was sitting in the back of the plane with 27 others, and he was sitting next to a flight attendant, perhaps Mrs. Lyles, I'm not sure. But the plane began to fly erratically, and he was aware that this was a situation that was not a normal hijacking situation, and he informed the operator that he knew that he was not going to make it out of this. His next response was to ask her to say the Lord's Prayer with him, and then he asked Jesus to help him. And once he got that guidance, he asked her to contact me—gave her my name and phone number and my children's names—and to tell us how much he loved us.

"And then once he had all that business squared away, he did what Todd would normally do, and he took some action, and what he did was he told the operator that he and some other people on the flight were deciding to jump on the hijacker with the bomb. . . ."

"Were you surprised at anything Todd did?" King asked her.

"No. . . . He was a man of action and a man of thought, and he would think through decisions before he made them, and he would seek wise counsel. I think he sought wise counsel, certainly in calling on Jesus and saying the Lord's Prayer and getting his heart right. . . . And after he sought that wise counsel, he was ready to take action. And that was the way he lived his life, based on faith and action, and that's the way he ended his life as well. . . . "

"You're not surprised, then, at the prayer either?"

"Not at all," she said. "Todd, like I said, was a man of faith. He knew that this life was not all there is, and this life was just here to prepare him for his eternity in heaven with God and with Jesus. And Todd made sure every day that he did his best. He wasn't perfect, and neither am I. But he did his best to make sure that he was living a life that was pleasing to God and that would help him know God better, and he acted on that all the way to the end, and I'm so proud."

She went on to say, "People sometimes look at me, I think, and wonder, is she in shock, is she, you know, unrealistic about what the situation is, and they don't see me all the other times when I'm, you know, breaking down and losing my composure. But, certainly, the faith that I have is like Todd's, and it's helping me understand the bigger picture here and that God's justice will ultimately prevail and that we have more to look forward to than just what we see here around us on earth."

Larry King's facial expression and riveted attention made it clear that at this point he was unusually moved. And it was his concluding remarks that proved the power of Lisa's unflinching trust in Jesus: "I admire your faith and your courage. You've given a lot of people a lot of hope here tonight. You're an extraordinary lady, Lisa, and we wish you luck, and we hope to see you again soon." [1]

Count on it, having interviewed thousands of people through the years, his words were not just polite expressions of condolence. He was deeply touched.

Jesus showed up in strength that night on national television. On the platform of great personal tragedy, the kind that would normally overwhelm non-Jesus people with deep despair and hopelessness, Lisa proved that Jesus works even in the worst of times. The "good works" of unflinching trust and confidence caught the attention of a watching world. Good theology is often expressed best in action and attitude.

⁓

In Jesus' terms, it was salt and light in action. Lisa had engaged a hostile society with the salt and light of her life..

Cracking the code of what it means to be salt is not difficult. When Jesus says, "If the salt has lost its savor," He underscores the reality that salt has the power to make a difference. In the ancient world salt was used to flavor, preserve, and purify. In Jesus' world, just mentioning salt would have meant that He was talking about something of great value. In fact, soldiers and others in Christ's day were often paid in salt—which explains the old saying, "He's not worth his salt."

As a flavor enhancer, salt adds zest and brings taste to what would otherwise be bland and disappointing. I love the metaphor. Salting our world means we are to avoid being grumpy, stagnated, out-of-date, and stodgy. We tend toward that at times. Unfortunately, soon after Christianity became the accepted religion of the Roman Empire something got lost in the victory. After observing Christians, Emperor Julian lamented, "Have you looked at these Christians closely? Hollow-eyed, pale-cheeked, flat-breasted, they brood their lives away unspurred by ambition. The sun shines for them, but they don't see it. The earth offers them its fullness, but they desire it not. All their desire is to renounce and suffer that they may come to die."[2]

The American editor, cynic, and libertarian, H. L. Mencken, once observed, "The chief charge of Protestantism to human thought is its massive proof that God is a bore."[3]

God help us!

As a friend of mine says, "If you have joy inside, you should have your heart telephone your face and let it know."

What would your world look like if you were salting it?

As salt we should season our world with the celebratory, confident, opti-mistic, and joyous nature of our position and privileges in Jesus. Because of all we have in Jesus, life is rich and free. By contrast, ultimately, life without Jesus is hollow, tasteless, and an empty pursuit. Our mission is to engage a world that has gone flat on itself with the zest and added value that Jesus brings to life.

Relationships will be blessed when salty followers are present. No one should laugh more deeply, listen more intently, prove that life is worth living more forthrightly, than we who follow Jesus. When fallen lives intersect ours, they should sense the depth of joy and purpose that only Jesus brings.

Not only do we advance the cause of Jesus by flavoring our world with His presence, but, like salt, we act as preservers as well. The drift toward deca-dence should be checked because followers of Jesus are present. Being salt means that we are better citizens who influence public policy, sit on school boards, occupy judicial benches, vote regularly, and speak out humbly yet clearly about morality and justice.

Our place of employment should be a better place because we are there encouraging our colleagues and putting in an honest day's work. People should trust us more because we are always true to our word. People should sense that there can be purpose and hope in life because they see it in us.

Followers who are keen on engaging their world with the salt of their lives measure their success in these terms. If you are truly salt, your family, friends, neighbors, and colleagues will feel that their lives are safer, purer, more pro-tected against evil, and a little brighter because you are there.

How do you score?

The better you score, the more interested others will be in hearing what you have to say about Jesus, the source of your "salt."

Light, on the other hand reveals, enlightens, guides, illuminates, and clar-ifies. Light is consistently victorious over the darkness. When Jesus said that light is like a city set on a hill that cannot be hidden, He underscored the fact that light is unique, observable, and penetrates the darkness.

When Jesus said, "In the same way, let your light shine before men, that they may see your good deeds and praise your Father in heaven" (Matthew 5:16 NIV), He was making it clear that lighting our night is not about our words or our conformity to rules and traditions. It is about the good deeds that extend the love of Jesus in tangible ways to those in need around our lives. The true light is a life-related reality that non-Jesus people actually experience.

Light bearers put skin on the claims of Jesus and show a watching world what God is really like.

How will you know when you are lighting your world? When there is something so unique and observable about the way you live that you catch the attention of a watching world! Your compelling and attractive life will snag the curiosity of others, who will wonder, What is that they have that is missing in my life?

You will know you are lighting up your world

- when you are no longer satisfied to simply be light within the four walls of your home or church;
- when you engage your world with intentional, sometimes sacrificial, and concrete acts of love that meet the needs of people you come in contact with;
- when your life remains uncompromised, so that the uniqueness of Jesus is never muddled or confused with the darkness;
- when your life so reflects the glory of God that others join you in living to glorify Him as well.

Lighting your night is about having a life so well lived that it is hard to deny the validity of what you say about Jesus and His claims.

In an earlier book I reflected on the power of a light-filled life clearly exhibited at the Presidential Prayer Breakfast in Washington, D.C. Mother

Teresa was the speaker. She made her way feebly to the rostrum over which her bent posture made her difficult to see. Seated to her right were Vice-President Gore and his wife, while to her left, on the other side of the podium, sat President Clinton and the First Lady. In front of these who had tried to use the power of the highest offices in our land to strengthen the cause of abortion, she said:

> I feel that the greatest destroyer of peace today is abortion, because it is war against the child, a direct killing of the innocent child, murder by the mother herself. . . . By abortion the mother does not learn to love, but kills even her own child to solve her problems. And, by abortion, the father is told that he does not have to take any responsibility at all for the child he has brought into the world. That father is likely to put other women into the same trouble. So abortion just leads to more abortion. Any country that accepts abortion is not teaching its people to love, but to use any violence to get what they want. This is why the greatest destroyer of love and peace is abortion.[4]

The crowd rose to its feet in applause while the Clintons and the Gores sat in silence throughout the thunderous ovation.

As President Clinton rose to address the group, he said of Mother Teresa, "It's hard to argue with a life so well lived." The world's most powerful advocate of abortion had little to say in the face of a life characterized by the compelling outcomes of good works. While I have some theological differences with Mother Teresa, I must say that my heart rejoiced at the power of her compelling acts of righteousness. Her words carried more weight as a result of her good works.

Is there anything about your life that is so well lived that others find that your consistent good works validate your words about Jesus? Lighting your non-Jesus world is about having a life that is "so well lived"!

What we cannot miss is that both salt and light are only effective when they engage their surroundings. Salt left in the shaker is of no use. In fact, Jesus reminds us, if it is left to itself for too long, it loses its potency and there is no hope for it to regain its use. And light is of no use when it is covered up.

We have no choice but to accept the challenge of salting and lighting our world.

I wonder if we are really ready to embrace this agenda. For too long, American Christianity has not engaged our world. It has been primarily about us. Our best sellers are consistently books on how to enhance our personal relationship with Christ; how to solve our family problems and money woes; how to study the Bible and glean deeper truths; how to build bigger and better churches; and how to pray more often and with greater power. Aside from a periodic bestseller by Chuck Colson or Ravi Zacharias, there are comparatively few books that push us beyond ourselves to the commission of Jesus to engage our world.

I need to be clear here. Slow down and absorb what I am about to say. It needs to sink to the depths of your consciousness in a soulish way. This call to salt and light our world insists that we get beyond ourselves and our cloisters and intentionally connect with our world on His behalf.

This point cannot be taken lightly. Comprehending its vast, profound ramifications lays claim to the entirety of our lives and will catapult us beyond the gripes, petty issues, and personal preferences that so often derail us.

❧

She stood in line long after the service to talk to me. I could see her coming out of the corner of my eye and knew that she had something urgent on her mind. She did. At least it was urgent to her.

She and her husband were thinking about leaving the church. When I asked why, she rather sanctimoniously informed me that their pastor had joined a country club. I happen to know the pastor well. He serves a very large and growing church and lives with all the typical stresses that go with that kind of calling. He is an avid golfer and finds that the brief seasons of getting away "to visit the Greens" are therapeutic for him. She went on to stack the deck against him by saying that her husband had found many verses in the Bible that proved her pastor was biblically wrong (I doubted it, but didn't challenge her on that point). To top it off, a neighbor told her that the pastor in question had been seen having brunch at the club with his family the previous Sunday morning. And, she said rather indignantly, "Why wasn't he in church?" Well, the church where he is the pastor has a Saturday night service. Since he was on vacation at the time, and knowing him, it's my guess that he went to church the evening before.

I mentioned to the concerned woman that the church was doing a splendid job of impacting its community for Jesus and that the test of a worthy church is probably decided on a different plane than where the pastor plays golf. I encouraged her to raise her perspectives to the higher issues of advancing Christ in our world. In fact I suggested that we should be pleased that such an articulate follower of Jesus could take the light to club members who need Jesus. She replied that Jesus would have taken His light to the streets, to those in poverty and despair. She totally ignored the reality that Jesus' love also covers country club golfers who stand in need of His grace.

The conversation is typical of the kind of insipid, downgraded, embarrassing stuff that occurs when followers forget we are called to the task of getting beyond ourselves and engaging our world. When church is only about us and our preferences, we invariably implode on ourselves.

Getting serious about engaging our world means that we need to mark the pitfalls that so often disable advocates for Jesus. One challenge is the problem of becoming assimilated into the world. The early church often struggled with losing its uniqueness and becoming too much like its environment. As you probably know, the problem with the Christians in Corinth was that

there was too much of Corinth in the Christians. In our day as well, assimilation threatens to take the punch out of our saltiness. Jesus warned that we might
become so lax that our salt loses its flavor and becomes useless. Salt without
flavor forecasts the danger of our becoming just like the world in which we live!
In other words, from Jesus' point of view, we add no value to our world. Countless numbers of us are like that. Aside from the fact that we go to church and
keep a few particular rules, others would never know the difference. We gossip,
complain, and otherwise sin with the best of them. Be warned: assimilation is
an ever-present danger. As someone well said, "If you were accused of being
a Christian would there be enough evidence to convict you?"

Jesus also warns that light can be rendered of no effect by our isolation.
His warning that we dare not put the light under a bushel was a clear signal
that He knew our tendency to betray the light by shielding it from those who
need it most. And His command that we let it shine "before men" so that "they
may see your good works" distinctly defines our lives as light that refuses to
exist in isolation. Beware of the comfortable confines of disconnected Christianity—of small groups, choirs, committees, and the business of His work
in church world. His work is to take the Light of the World to our world. Don't
be confused.

When Jesus called His disciples to salt and light their world, the really
"good people" were anything but engaged with their world. In fact, they actually felt quite good about their disengagement. Their disconnect would have
been articulately defended as "true religion." Which only raises a huge caution flag. Feeling good about how you do as a Christian is no guarantee that
Jesus is pleased.

A quick look at the "good people" of Jesus' day helps us to take note of
disabling pitfalls. As you read about them, do not confine them to the box of

history. See if there is anything of "you" in their shortcomings. They shame-lessly lived out their disengagement and isolation in four distinct ways.

⤶

The Essenes totally withdrew from society and gave their lives to the preservation of Scripture. They lived in tightly bound communities with no contact to the outside world and particularly no contact with the hostile pagan-ism of their day. Their report card for engaging the culture? "F"!

In fact, they were so disengaged they believed that no one who was lame, blind, or otherwise maimed would qualify to enter the kingdom. Their laws of purity would not allow it. We could be highly critical of this approach if it weren't for the fact that many of us who call ourselves by His name are just about this disengaged. We know very few unbelievers. We stay in our safe, comfortable clusters and resist opportunities to interact with our pagan world. We pass on office parties. Invitations to dinners or events where we may feel a little uncomfortable are often refused. Our neighbors see little of us because we find it easier to spend more time at church and with our "friends" than we do engaging the guy next door. It's hard to be effective as light when you spend most of your time in the lighthouse with light keepers.

⤶

Unlike the Essenes, the Pharisees lived in communities that were well mixed with Jews and Gentiles. They had many opportunities to turn on the lights. Unfortunately, they kept flipping the wrong switch. For them, the most important way to let their light shine was to create a community identity based on keeping the rules. They had, as you probably know, all the rules, codes, and traditions down to a habit and were the 24-7-365 behavior police. Their intent was to be known by their rules and their strict adherence to them.

Rules were a means whereby they maintained Jewish identity. Good Jews obeyed the rules. Bad people didn't. It was just as simple as that. This all-consuming attitude separated them from the world they were called to engage. Tax collectors, sinners, and prostitutes found no door of mercy or grace through which to pass. Philo observes that the Pharisees were "full of zeal for the laws, strictest guardians of the ancestral traditions . . . who have their eyes upon transgressors and are merciless to those who subvert the laws."[5]

The Pharisees were violently opposed to Jesus for many reasons. High on the list was that while honoring the "real rules" He refused to give in to the oppressive rules that elevated the traditions of the Pharisees above the needs of people. Jesus was so dedicated to salting and lighting His world that He often engaged the bad people of His day on their turf. He defined "the light" as much more than a code of rules. The light was for those bound in darkness, and Jesus relentlessly illuminated those who needed it most.

It irritated the Pharisees to no end that Jesus lived a celebrant kind of life; feasting and dining with all kinds of people, while they practiced fasting, self-denial, and separation from sinners—the attitudes and behavior they wrongfully thought defined true spirituality.

If you are wondering if there is a parallel . . . think carefully. For generations, we have tended to elevate "rule-keeping" to the extent that it became the primary test of true-blue followers. Some of our rules were not then, nor are they now, explicitly biblical. Instead, they are, at times, man-made restrictions crafted to cover all the contingencies of living in a dark world so that earnest Christians are kept from getting too close to danger. The problem with these "extended" rules is that they isolate us from engaging a world that desperately needs our light. When we don't understand our true mission, we easily believe that conformity to church expectations is more important than engaging our world.

Don't get me wrong, righteousness is vitally important and "real rules" are indispensable. But they are not the primary means by which we engage our world. Our connecting identity is that we are Jesus' people who intentionally engage the world with the reality of His love and truth.

We would do well to identify those codes, traditions, and preferences that inhibit our capacity to relate effectively to non-Jesus friends, family, and neighbors. It's important to ask ourselves if the prohibitions that keep us from engaging are clearly biblical or are more a matter of tradition and preference. If they are not unmistakably demanded in Scripture, then they may at times need to be set aside if they get in the way of the greater good of relating biblically to those around us.

The issues will differ for all of us. I remember talking with a student who wondered if it was right to go to the bar with the guys he worked with. He had been trying to build significant relationships with them but realized that the relationships were developed after work at the local watering hole. I know of individuals who minister to gays and as a part of that ministry find that the neediest are often hanging out in gay bars. Should they go and find them there? What should you do if your neighbors finally ask you over for dinner and offer you a glass of wine as an act of hospitality? Or what should you do with the bottle of wine they bring over as a gift of appreciation when you ask them over for an evening in your home?

Would you miss church to go fishing with your colleague at work? Should you dance with your new daughter-in-law at your son's wedding when the MC calls the new father-in-law for the next dance? Should unchurched attendees at the reception be given the opportunity to wonder why you would refuse the normal courtesy of the next dance? Or, what should you do if when playing golf with three non-believing friends, they want to play for a small amount of "prize money" on each hole?

What message will we bring to the nonbelieving world? Will it be the message of our preferences and traditions or the liberating, lightbearing message of Jesus as Savior and Lord?

Granted, engaging our world will challenge our values and beliefs.

Temptations are greater, discernment more necessary, and life is generally less predictable. Life is easier inside the salt shaker and far less challenging underneath the bushel. But the moment we get serious about engaging our world in effective ways for Jesus' sake, the risks get higher and neatly packaged answers disappear. Not everyone will understand and you may take some heat from your own troops. But the issue is critical. In what ways can you connect with the lives around you and still keep a clear conscience and pure heart? Jesus scandalized His religious world because He hung out with all the wrong people. But, as He said, He came to seek and to save that which was lost.

As one New Testament scholar has observed, Jesus fell out with the Pharisees precisely because His "kingdom-agenda for Israel demanded that Israel leave off her frantic and paranoid self-defense, reinforced as it now was by the ancestral codes, and embrace instead the vocation to be the light of the world, the salt of the earth."

~

The Zealots fell into the third trap of disengagement. They were singularly focused on the overthrow of the Roman occupation. The freedom fighters of their day, they were ready to engage the pagan Romans at a moment's notice. If they were here today, they would probably wear fatigues with a Star of David proudly displayed on the shoulder. The Roman occupation was not to be tolerated, and all of them were willing to spill their blood in the streets for the cause. They were dedicated to restoring Israel to its rightful place of independence and honor through sharpened sword wielded in righteous determination.

In our day, bombers of abortion clinics would qualify as modern-day Zealots, as would all the rest of us who are just flat-out mad about the sin and rebellion that goes unchecked in our culture. I have felt for a long time that the church in America is far better at venting our consternation than we are at practicing compassion and caring for the lost souls of the "occupiers."

Noticing the rapid slouch toward Gomorrah, we have spoken angry words, pointed self-righteous fingers, and written fiery volumes against purveyors of decline. The whining and grumbling index registers dangerously high when we talk about having lost our precious America. Don't get me wrong. I agree with the bumper sticker that says, "If you're not outraged you're not paying attention!" But we are to be among those who have learned to be angry without sinning and who don't let the sun go down on our wrath. In fact, the mark of our followership is that we love our enemies (Matthew 5:43–48).

I fear that we have embarrassed ourselves and betrayed the heart of God by being so long on mad and so short on mercy. With our spirits in a snit, we have often appeared to our world as just another irritated subgroup demanding our way with raised fists.

Let's admit it, Jesus had a better plan for engaging a dark and dying world.

Interestingly enough, the compelling person and message of Jesus captured the heart of one of these street warriors and transitioned his focus from violence to a message of engagement; from anger and war to a message of peace, mercy, and love. His name was Simon the Zealot. He is listed among the twelve disciples.

It is important to note in the ministry of Jesus that while He was clear about sin and repentance, He never expressed anger toward the pagans in the environment. When He expressed His anger, it was reserved for religious folk who oppressed God's people with their greed and burdensome rules. It was the hypocrisy of religious leaders and their distortion of true godliness that ignited the wrath of Jesus—a thought well worth a moment of reflection for those of us who consider ourselves "good people" with "appropriate" disdain for a decadent culture.

As true followers we are to be salt and light, not an angry mob.

Lastly, the Herodians and the chief priests engaged their world, but did it through compromise and acquiescence to the power structure of that day. Herod could only enjoy temporal power and prosperity as long as he cooperated with Rome. The chief priests—the leaders of the synagogue—held their lucrative positions with the blessings of Rome. They gained everything they wanted but in the process had lost their capacity to be salt and light.

Countless numbers of modern-day Christians have not wanted to hibernate or to be bound by a multiplicity of rules. They have felt uncomfortable with those who always want to pick a fight with the world. Unfortunately these Christians have chosen to engage the world by embracing the world. Pleasures, self-satisfaction, and material comforts dominate their agenda. Life is more about their cars and clubs than about the good works that emanate from a unique reflection of the character and purity of Jesus. These Herodian types rarely think "kingdom" thoughts and live as though this is the only world there is. The radical calling of Jesus rarely registers even though they are regular churchgoers and would classify themselves among the better people of our world.

It should not go unnoticed that Israel's great mistake was to assume that the pagan world around them was a target for the imminent judgment of God. With that in mind, the thought of engaging their world with the light and glory of God was simply not on their spiritual radar screen. However, through the Old Testament and into the time of Jesus, God's will was that Israel would glorify Him among the pagans. He never intended that they withdraw from their world and wait for its destruction. As a result of their failure to carry out God's plan, His judgment fell not on the Roman Empire but on Israel. In A.D. 70 Jerusalem was demolished in a devastating attack. They had failed in their mission to light their world by engaging it with God's power and grace.

N. T. Wright notes, "God's purpose would not after all be to vindicate Israel as a nation against the pagan hordes. . . . On the contrary, Jesus announced, increasingly clearly, that God's judgment would not fall on the surrounding nations, but on the Israel that had failed to be the light of the world."[6]

We dare not be content to sing the old gospel song, "This world is not my home, I'm just a' passin' through," as we anticipate with detached interest His judgment on our world. Jesus was anything but detached from His world. He cut a swath of salt and light that the world could not ignore. Christ brought the salt and life of His life to a needy culture even when it meant He had to die to accomplish the task.

When I was a boy in Sunday school we often sang, "This Little Light of Mine." One stanza went, "Hide it under a bushel?" at which point we would shout as loud as we could, "No! I'm going to let it shine." As the Scripture says, "A little child shall lead them" (Isaiah 11:6 KJV)! Amen!

This chapter taken from The Trouble With Jesus, *Moody Publishers, 2003*

M y father and grandfather preached into a culture that shared a basic
intellectual acceptance to the claims of Jesus. People in their churches
found that witnessing for Jesus at work or in their neighborhood at least had
the advantage of a general cultural awareness of God, Jesus, sin, heaven, and hell.
In their world, hostility to the gospel was much more subdued. In those days
people were more willing to listen to truths about Jesus and His claims.

For us it is different. In fact, in our culture words themselves get lost in the
meaningless maze of "whatever it means to you is fine." Gene Veith, in his insightful work, *Postmodern Times*, tells this story about the difficulty of verbal witness
into the postmodern mindset:

> Charles Colson tells a story about a dinner he had with a media per-
> sonality, and trying to talk with him about Christianity. Colson shared
> with him that he needed to come to Christ. "Obviously Jesus worked for
> you," his friend replied, but went on to tell him about someone he knew

whose life had been turned around by New Age spirituality. "Crystals, channeling—it worked for her. Just like your Jesus."

Colson tried to explain the difference, but got nowhere. He raised the issue of death and afterlife, but his friend did not believe in Heaven or Hell and was not particularly bothered by the prospect of dying.

Colson explained what the Bible said, but his friend did not believe in the Bible or any other spiritual authority.

Finally, Colson mentioned a Woody Allen movie, *Crimes and Misdemeanors*, about a killer who silences his conscience by concluding that life is nothing more than the survival of the fittest. The friend became thoughtful. Colson followed with examples from Tolstoy and C. S. Lewis on the reality of the moral law. The friend was following him. Then Colson cited the epistle of Romans on human inability to keep the law. His friend then paid close attention to the message of Christ's atoning work on the cross.

Although the friend did not become a Christian, Colson felt that he finally had broken through at least some of his defenses. The difficulty was in finding a common frame of reference. Because of his friend's mind-set, the usual evangelistic approaches didn't work. "My experience," says Colson, "is a sobering illustration of how resistant the modern mind has become to the Christian message. And it raises some serious questions about the effectiveness of traditional evangelistic methods in our age. For the spirit of the age is changing more quickly than many of us realize."[1]

Which brings us to this crucial question: How can you engage a world where very few are ready to come to grips with what you have to say? Especially if you know little about Woody Allen, Tolstoy, or C. S. Lewis?

This is not to say that speaking up for Jesus is not critically important. We have just learned how important it is. The point is that while speaking up for Jesus keeps the definitions clear and the issues in play, it is showing up for Jesus in the way we live that has the power to attract the curiosity of a watching world and to break up the hardpan soil of their hearts.

~☙~

Recently I received an e-mail from a new follower of Jesus who is learning how to live for Jesus in her non-Jesus world. She wrote,

> *I'm a relatively new Christian (6 months) . . . I was moved to tears at what you said. Since I became a Christian in the middle of the school year, it was very awkward for me, because my friends didn't understand all of the GREAT things that Jesus was doing in my life. I practically didn't understand either, but I was at peace, and I was ready to begin that walk as a Christian. It was actually my senior year math teacher, Michelle, that brought me to Harvest for the first time, and I've gone ever since and was saved shortly after that first time.*
>
> *Your message today meant so much to me, because I have a hard time really speaking up about Jesus. I know that I've been given numerous chances (friends will ask me for advice on a problem, and I try to help them out as much as I can). It's after those chances that I realize that I had a GREAT opportunity to tell them that they can turn to God when times are rough, and that He is the way that you will and can overcome ANYthing. This message really gave me the confidence to do just that. After hearing so many stories about others trying to dodge Jesus and speaking of Him . . . I realized that I should be proud to say that I am a follower of Jesus Christ, and He alone is all that I need. I don't need what everyone else says that I need. I need Him.*
>
> *I was also glad that you brought up the point that people can stop listening, but they don't stop watching. My teacher (the one who took me to Harvest) always had a "way about her." I could never figure out what it was . . . and now I know!!! I need to really live to have that "way about you" look for me as well!!!*

When Jesus commissions us to be light in our world, He makes it clear that there is a power more compelling than our words, which is important for all of us who have grown up in a Christian culture that thinks of evangelism in terms of words and verbal formulas. As we have noted, Jesus defines "light" as good works and informs us that the power of the light is in what people see in our lives.

Since "good works" are a critically important part of impacting our non-Jesus world, let's slow down a little and look closely at how you can penetrate the darkness around you with the marvelous light of Jesus expressed through the way you live.

⸰❧

You may be experiencing a surge of resistance when you hear another demand for good works in your life. Let me ease your pain. Any thought that the light is about a stifling, oppressive, legalistic, performance-based, rule-preeminent Christianity is not what Jesus had in mind.

For which I am personally glad.

Let me pause here to let you in on a secret. Sometimes I get tired of being good. Not tired of Jesus. Not tired of the work of the Spirit, just tired of having to be good. Having grown up a pastor's son and then being a pastor myself and now having served as president of a Christian college, I know what it's like to live in the fishbowl of expectations—always having to be good.

In my worst moments I'd like to do something to shock people. Nothing unrighteous and immoral—I am well aware of how destructive that would be—but something slightly outside the lines for a change. Fortunately, when these feelings get running too high, the Spirit tells me to relax and stay in the big picture of what is best in the long run. Nevertheless, we all know how burdensome and sometimes seemingly boring rules can be if they are kept simply because it is the thing "proper" Christians do.

Thankfully, being good is far more strategic than just doing "the proper thing."

The Greeks had several words for "good" in their language. The two used most often in the New Testament are *agathos* and *kalos*. *Agathos* generally refers to good in the sense of being morally upright. A respectable, honest person who lives within biblical boundaries is *agathos*. Growing Christians should be increasingly *agathos* in every area of life. But not just to be good for goodness' sake.

There are a multitude of reasons why we must be good (*agathos*) as followers of Christ.

In Psalm 1 it is clear that delighting in God's law and meditating in it day and night leads to a blessed life. Indeed! A blessed life is a life without haunting guilt, fear, loss of self-esteem, and all the other destructive baggage sin produces. It's no wonder that in Psalm 19:7–10 the psalmist revels in the fact that the law of God restores the soul and the testimonies of the Lord make the simple wise. He reminds us that the fear of the Lord makes us clean and the judgments of the Lord are true. So taken is he with the benefits and blessings of the "good life," that he exclaims of God's laws: "They are more desirable than gold, yes, than much fine gold; sweeter also than honey and the drippings of the honeycomb."

Goodness of life also has value in that it brings pleasure to the One we love. Righteousness is a worship language that enables us to express to Jesus how much we love and adore Him.

Peter was aware of the protection that *agathos* brings to our lives when he warned, "I urge you . . . to abstain from fleshly lusts which wage war against the soul" (1 Peter 2:11). Sin patterns in our lives, whether public or private, leave our soul vulnerable to Satan's attack.

And that is no little matter. Your soul is the essence of who you are. It is where God meets you. It is where all of life is planned and programmed. For a Christian, it is a fortified stronghold of spiritual vitality. It is where you draw strength to serve and glorify God. There is no more important part of your being than your soul. It is the real you.

A life that rejects the call of goodness and gives in to the flesh lets the drawbridge down, permitting the Enemy to storm the gates and wage a war that, when successful, discourages, dismantles, and destroys the inner work of God in our lives. And although most of us apply enough discipline to maintain a proper appearance on the outside, the truth is that a life given over to its own out-of-bounds desires is a life where the soul has been plundered and pillaged and as such is void of spiritual power!

Most important, in the context of our commitment to engage our world with Jesus, being morally upright gives credibility to our claims as followers of Jesus. It builds a platform on which the good works of our lives can be seen without the accusation of hypocrisy clouding the view. Not only does hypocrisy in our lives bother God, it gives a watching world an excuse to reject Jesus.

If our lives are not morally consistent with what we claim to be good and true, there is no hope of catching the attention of those in our lives. They will be too turned off to notice. People everywhere are desperately searching for something that is real. Something they can believe in that is solid, true, and satisfying. They want something that works. If we betray what we say is true by denying it in our lives, they will look elsewhere.

On one occasion when defending a friend against the attack of a group of "do-gooders," Harry Truman said, "In times past he owned a bawdy house, a saloon and gambling establishment . . . but he's all man. I wonder who is worth more in the sight of the Lord, he or the sniveling church members who weep on Sunday, play with whores on Monday, drink on Tuesday, sell out to the Boss on Wednesday, repent about Friday and start over again on Sunday?"[2]

Don't dismiss the acidic comment as a typical "give-'em-hell" Truman moment.

When Truman was a teenager, he had a job at the local drugstore in his hometown. As such he was privy to a lot of town chatter and had an inside view of the behavior of some of Independence's leading citizens. One of the memories Truman had of those early days were the times when certain folk came into the store and went behind the counter for a clandestine downing of gin. He remembered them getting their drinks and then sliding money across the counter for him to put into the till. Unfortunately, these stealth-imbibers were leading lights in the local church and, in fact, the founders of the local chapter of the Temperance Union.[3]

This sort of blatant hypocrisy disengages the power of any good works we might do. But beware of the hypocrisy that is more subtly expressed in our attitudes. Our Christianity too often comes off as rigid, snooty, self-serving arrogance.

As one author notes, Christianity is often "a refuge for smug hypocrites who preach love of neighbor but practice adoration of self, who revile riches in public while plundering their neighbors the rest of the week, and who extol charity, sexual restraint and self-sacrifice, but are loathe to practice these virtues themselves. These Christians pay lip service to the Gospel but never embrace its fundamental message."[4]

Not exactly what Jesus had in mind when He called us to be lights of the world.

But as important as *agathos* is, it is rarely a compelling feature in drawing others to Jesus. It supports our claim that morality counts and gives us credibility as being consistent and satisfied. But the truth remains that while your average pagan may respect you for your good behavior, he probably doesn't find a heavy dose of *agathos* real attractive for himself. Try telling your unsaved neighbor that if he becomes a Christian he could begin to tithe! He most likely is less than interested in regular church attendance. He may actually like getting a little drunk now and then. A brief overnight fling or a lie to get himself out of trouble are among the things he might not want to give up. Most pagans would like the freedom to swear now and then on the golf course and to snoop around on the Internet after hours. So while being *agathos* is vitally important for us, it is not the key to drawing the hearts of a watching world to Jesus.

Which brings us to the good works that do have the power to open hearts to the message of Jesus.

~&

When Jesus speaks of good works as the definition of our being the light of our world, *kalos* is the word that is used (Matthew 5:16).

Kalos is goodness in the sense of doing good things. The word most often casts goodness in terms of what is excellent, attractive, powerful, helpful, admirable, or well done.

In the context of "light," *kalos* is doing things consistent with what Jesus would do. Even a casual reading of the gospel of John reminds us that His good works aroused the curiosity of the multitudes and provided an opportunity to proclaim the good news of the kingdom.

In order to understand the impact of "*kalos* works," we need to put *kalos* and *agathos* in perspective. To be *agathos* means that if you walk down the street and pass the local porn shop you quicken your pace and look the other way. But if in the next block you see a shivering street person in front of a Starbucks begging for enough money to buy a cup of coffee, and you continue on your way without giving thought to his need, you have failed to be *kalos*. In fact, if your heart is not moved to pray for the spiritual needs of those in the porn shop whose lives are cascading into destruction, then you have failed to be *kalos* as well.

You could be the best rule keeper in town, but if you cringe and cold-shoulder the well-pierced counter-culture person who comes into your church, you have failed to be *kalos*. *Kalos* may not require that you like everything about a person, but it does demand that you receive him as another sinner in need —much like yourself—who has come within the sound of the good news.

SHOWING UP FOR HIM

Agathos is about rules . . . *kalos* is about relationships.

Agathos behaves . . . *kalos* blesses others.

Agathos does what is right . . . *kalos* forgives those who don't. Without exception.

Agathos tithes . . . *kalos* gives above the tithe to those in need with no thought of receiving in return.

Agathos may not do what others at the office do . . . *kalos* keeps a keen eye out at the office for opportunities to express the love of Jesus to fellow workers.

Kalos lights your world with attention-getting works that arouse the curiosity of a watching world.

You can't "do" Jesus in your non-Jesus world without it.

Which explains why Peter, in a letter written to followers spread far and wide in the hostile and decadent pagan world of the Roman Empire, put the *kalos* principle into the heart of his strategy for living for Jesus in a non-Jesus world.

To the marginalized, suffering followers he said, "Keep your behavior excellent among the Gentiles, so that in the thing in which they slander you as evildoers, they may because of your good deeds [*kalos*], as they observe them, glorify God in the day of visitation" (1 Peter 2:12).

As Peter noted, the early believers were often slandered "as evildoers." As we have noted, the enemies of the followers of Jesus spread rumors that their communion dinners were orgies, and since it was known that in their communion ritual they drank the blood of Christ and ate His flesh, they were criticized as "cannibals." Because of their demand for uncompromised commitment to Jesus over all earthly allegiances, they were despised for being antifamily. They were also slandered as enemies of the state for refusing to claim, "Caesar is lord."

So, given their bad press, how could they ever take the good news past the thresholds of their house churches?

177

They engaged their world with the light of the "*kalos*-power" of their good works.

A few verses earlier, Peter wrote that believers are to "proclaim the excellencies of Him who has called you out of darkness into His marvelous light" (v. 9). The proclamation of the excellencies of Christ, he explains three verses later, are the observable *kalos* works of our lives.

The word picture in this text is fabulous. We have been brought from our own darkness into His light. And being in His marvelous light, we are to show off what He is like to a watching world. It is as though we have been called from the darkness of the back stage of our sin and alienation from God into the spotlight of His grace. The curtain parts and it is now your turn to do your part in showing off the reality of Jesus.

Peter makes an interesting point about life in the spotlight. He notes that "spotlighting" is particularly effective with people who have come to the end of themselves. He notes in verse 12 that observers will come to glorify God in the day of their "visitation." This is a word that is often used of the judgment of God for sin. Most scholars agree that Peter is not referring here primarily to the final judgment but to the present judgment that people experience when they live life without Him. The Bible is clear—and life validates the point—that life lived in an immoral, godless way feels the guilt, brokenness, bankruptcy, despair, and hopelessness that life without God ultimately brings. It's like Douglas Coupland, the author who coined the term "Generation X," said. My secret is that I need God—that I am sick and can no longer make it alone. At this point, it's the reality of Jesus in the lives of people they know that strikes a chord of hope.

You know it's working when someone asks, "I've been watching your life. What is it that you have that I don't ever seem to be able to find?" And then we can say, "Let me tell you about Jesus."

⤳

My friend Paul Eschelman, founder of The Jesus Film project, recently told me a riveting story.

He was meeting with a group of advertising executives from a major Hollywood film company. They were discussing global marketing strategies for a new release of The Jesus Film. The senior executive was a Jewish man who had an immense profile in the movie industry. After the meeting, the senior executive asked Paul if he had a moment to meet with him privately in his office. Paul was surprised and of course gladly complied.

As they sat down, the marketing mogul began telling Paul about his life. He and his wife had sometime ago gone through a very serious health problem with their child. One day he noticed their live-in housemaid kneeling in her room in prayer. Later, he asked what she was praying for. She replied, "Your child, that God might be gracious to heal her." She went on to say that she had been praying for the child for days. In fact, she added, she prayed for the whole family every day. The film marketer was deeply moved and asked if she would come to the door each morning and pray a blessing over him and his wife as they left for work.

A few months later, his wife became seriously ill with breast cancer. With his wife at death's door, he walked down the street to find consolation at his synagogue. Discovering that it was bingo night, he kept walking and found a church with its doors open. He went in and met the pastor in the sanctuary. As he poured out his grief, the pastor prayed with him and assured him of his concern.

The next morning, when he went to visit his wife in the hospital, the doctor turned to him and said, "I thought you were Jewish?"

"I am!"

"Oh," the doctor replied. "Then why was a pastor sitting and praying at your wife's bedside through most of the night?"

As Paul sat listening, deeply intrigued, the man then said, as tears filled his eyes, "Our maid passed away this week. And now I have no one to get me to God. Can you help me?"

Paul said, "Can I tell you about Jesus?" To which he replied, "Of course!"

Before Paul left the office, the powerful executive had prayed to receive Christ as his Savior.

I should hasten to add that spotlighting may not always turn out so well. Not everyone responded to the good works Jesus did. In fact, His good works only made His enemies more determined to extinguish His light. But though not all will respond, some will.

What I love about Paul's story is that it was the *kalos* power of the good works of two faithful followers that opened the door for an otherwise resistant heart to hear the good news of Jesus. God used two spotlight players to lead a non-Jesus person to the light. Nothing spectacular, just two ordinary people taking the opportunity to *kalos* their world.

A pastor friend of mine serves in a California town that is without doubt among the most culturally radical communities in America. As he says, "It makes Berkeley look like a Sunday school picnic." For instance, you can walk down the street and see posters announcing séances that help you get in touch with departed spirits, and seminars to help you learn how to cast a spell on your enemies. Needless to say, Christians have not been held in high esteem. In fact they were an outright despised minority. It was hard for churches to get planning permissions, building permits, or any other normal benefits from the town fathers.

My friend tells me of many Pastors' Fellowship meetings where the topic of conversation was consumed with how difficult ministry was in their town. Whining about the awful environment characterized their gatherings. Tired of the negative tone of the meetings, one pastor suggested they pray about how they might be able to reach their town in spite of the hostility.

Brilliant!

They decided to engage their community with the salt-and-light agenda.

AIDS is a huge problem in their area. One of the churches established a ministry to AIDS victims. Individuals in other churches with medical and compassion service backgrounds engaged the elderly to spotlight Christ's love to many who were dying lonely and rejected. Another church chose to minister to the homeless; another to single mothers; another to pregnant teens; and another to kids at risk. The stage was full of spotlighters.

And though it wasn't an overnight win, in time their seacoast town began to notice that the Jesus people were bringing healing and help. Town fathers and social agencies began to call on the churches for volunteers, advice, and support. The churches were looked on as a part of the solution to the problems that inevitably come from life without God. In the day of "visitation," followers of Jesus showed up and by their observable works of light began to win the hearts of their fiercest enemies. Today, although not everyone in town has become a follower, the once-cowering churches are growing with a fresh vibrancy. And now it's a lot easier to get building permits.

⁓

A friend came to me recently and asked what I would do differently if I were to go back to the pastorate.

The answer came quickly.

I would want to revolutionize the "status quo" mind-set of those who claim to be faithful followers of Jesus. Most of us have thought that being a good Christian is about accepting Christ, embracing and defending sound doctrine, keeping the rules, and in our best moments cultivating a relationship with Jesus. And while all of this is vital, it's not the total package.

If I could pull up a chair beside you right now, I would want to look in your eyes and tell you how pivotally important my next words are. Listen carefully. Authentic Christianity is not just about keeping and protecting the faith and keeping the rules. It is even more than living to deepen your relationship with Jesus. Authentic Christianity, the real deal, is about embracing all of these important elements and using them as a resource to actively and intentionally engage your world with acts of love that show off Jesus.

Anything short of this is a denial of His intentions for those of us who follow Him. If we don't actively engage our world on His behalf, we have fallen short of following Him. For if you follow Him, He will ultimately take you right to the needs of those around you. It is obvious to even the most casual observer that He came to effectively engage His world, not to hibernate with His chosen few.

In fact, you and I are redeemed and heaven bound because of His passion to engage our needs in the face of great hostility. The least we can do, as a debt of love, is to go and do the same for others. That is exactly what He commissioned us to do when He said, "As the Father has sent me, I am sending you" (John 20:21 NIV).

If I had one more opportunity to shepherd a flock, my desire would be to equip and mobilize His followers to engage our community—through programs, personal relationships, and casual encounters —with the brilliance of His light. Church was never intended to be an exclusive club focused inward. In fact, some of the truest forms of Christianity—terms of engagement— are often expressed outside the context of church. Who was it that said so appropriately, "The church is one of the few organizations to exist for the benefit of its nonmembers as well as its members"?

Real Christians work to build relationships into which they can pour the *kalos* power of Jesus. We must take the love of Jesus to our neighbors, to the afflicted and the poor . . . to the needs of those you work with and to the stranger who happens to cross your path.

And when they ask you why you have blessed them, tell them Jesus sent you!

Carl Henry writes, "Can we take a holy initiative in history? Can we once more strike an apostolic stride? Can we put an ungodly world on the defensive again? Can we show men the folly of opposing Him who has already overcome the world, of rejecting fellowship with the coming King? Will we offer civilization a realistic option, or only a warning of impending doom? Will Christianity speak only to man's fears and frustrations, or will it also fill the vacuums in his heart and crown his longings for life at its best?"[5]

The answer must be yes.

Are you ready to change your mind about what it means to be an authentic follower of Jesus . . . to repent of a life focused on your own agendas and start the wonderful adventure of life lived according to His intentions? Will you join me in making a difference for Jesus in your world by committing your heart, energy, and resources to the power of taking *kalos* to needy hearts that cross your path every day?

Where and with whom will you start?

This chapter taken from The Trouble With Jesus, *Moody Publishers, 2003*

S hocking news interrupted a rather routine November morning on our campus: One of our recent graduates had been murdered in Lebanon. News of this magnitude takes a moment to sink in, but as it penetrated my heart, an unusual grief pressed on my spirit. Throughout the day, with its meetings, phone calls and issues, the ache in my heart kept reminding me that while the business of Moody Bible Institute continues, a great tragedy had occurred. Bonnie Witherall's death in the line of duty for Jesus Christ made the routine of my work seem small and petty by comparison to such terrible loss.

That evening I tried to assess why I felt so deeply about the news. Was it because I had heard the deep pain of her dad's sobs as I talked to him by phone? Was it because I knew her as a student and recalled many conversations with her husband whom she met at Moody? Could it have been the brutal way she was murdered in cold blood at point-blank range?

I wondered if my heart had been struck by the fact that the war on terrorism was no longer a headline but a wrenching reality—a too-close-to-home reality that had snuffed out an innocent life whose only crime was ministering to helpless refugees. Or was it that I love the vigor and passion that our students have for Jesus and His worldwide cause . . . and in a moment of unrestrained evil one of their lives was senselessly extinguished?

Perhaps it was pieces of all of the above. All I really knew was that in the dark region of the soul where what you know and how you feel get scrambled beyond recognition, I felt great sorrow and loss.

⁓

It was early in the morning when Bonnie went to the clinic to prepare for another day of touching poor Palestinian women with the love of Jesus. At that point, someone approached and, with premeditated intent, shot her three times in the head. She died instantly, leaving an equally dedicated husband behind with a lost love and dreams that would never be fulfilled. Bonnie was an intelligent and gifted young woman. She would have been successful at any endeavor had she stayed here in the United States. But the call of God gripped her heart, and she gave up normal comforts and great possibilities to take the good news of Jesus into harm's way.

While some may speculate that this was a senseless loss of life, and others will miss the privilege of peering deep into the wonder of this sorrow by second guessing, I, for one, want to go on record that Bonnie Witherall is my hero. She proved the hard fact that, increasingly, this evil world is not a friend to grace or truth. She reminds us that it is now more dangerous than ever to call ourselves Christian, particularly if we are willing to take His love into hostile environments. She demonstrates in a dramatic way that Jesus is not only worth living for, but dying for as well.

Bonnie, in death, has shown us the depth of the love of Jesus who put Himself in harm's way to be murdered in a cruel and unjust manner by people who could not tolerate His message. She is a modern-day martyr and as such joins a host in heaven who are especially honored, having done for Jesus what He willingly did for them 2,000 years ago.

All of us at Moody are deeply honored that we had the privilege of playing a part in preparing such a special person to serve her God in such a profound way.

We have lost a courageous and committed sister, and in this world that is no small thing.

I am reminded of Martin Luther's words about the value of fearless allegiance to God in the face of great evil...

And though this world, with devils filled,
Should threaten to undo us,
We will not fear, for God hath willed
His truth to triumph through us...
Let goods and kindred go.
This mortal life also.
The body they may kill; God's truth abideth still:
His Kingdom is forever!

This chapter taken from Moody *Magazine, January/February 2003*

FIVE

BEAUTIFUL SAVIOR

They say that the older you get, the better your long-term memory becomes, as your short-term memory declines. The other evening Martie and I were out for dinner with two other couples who all were older than we are. Frequently, one of us would begin a thought and then get stuck in a memory lapse about some name or place. In that awkward moment of silence as we struggled to call up the details, someone else would fill in the blank, and the conversation would go on.

It was then I realized that I was getting to the age when you need to travel in groups to get conversations done. Talking becomes a community affair. So I am getting the point about the short-term memory problem.

Recently, however, the long-term memory part of the deal has begun showing up in a wonderful way. Growing up as a pastor's son, I was at church for every service, which meant that I heard hymns and Christian songs sung repeatedly from my earliest days. It would be impressive had I kept track of how many times I sang those oft-repeated ones. And I have to confess that many of them soon became so commonplace that I could sing them with gusto while my mind was a thousand miles away, or on the pretty girl sharing the hymnal with me.

As church music changed, many of those hymns became ancient history . . . until recently. I find frequently, in just the right moments, lines from those songs of my past show up in my brain and focus my heart in encouraging and strengthening ways.

Not long ago I was struggling with one of those nagging temptations, when the words, *"Stoop to my weakness mighty as Thou art . . . and help me love thee as I ought to love!"* filled my heart with hope and help. Then directly on the heels of that the lyric, *"Spirit of the living God, fall afresh on me"* began to spin its tune as the prayer of my heart. God's grace in the moment had come in the form of song memories!

I have, in fact, found myself going into this newly discovered "song-file" often for inspiration and worship. Think of the strength in these words, *"Be still my soul! The Lord is on your side . . . In every change He faithful will remain."* Or of the important refocusing that this heart song brings to our lives, *"I need Thee, O I need Thee; every hour I need thee! O bless me now, my Savior—I come to Thee."*

In those days filled with disappointment and discouragement I need words like, *"Turn your eyes upon Jesus, Look full in His wonderful face, And the things of earth will grow strangely dim, in the light of His glory and grace."*

"And Lord haste the day when the faith shall be sight, the clouds be rolled back as a scroll: The trump shall resound, and the Lord shall descend, even so—it is well with my soul" reminds me that the day is coming when I will see Him face-to-face and the unspoiled joys of heaven will, by His grace, be mine. Sometimes the song-file kicks up a phrase that lifts my mind to a fresh glimpse of the wonder of my God.

In "Holy, Holy, Holy" God is described as "merciful and mighty." Did you ever wonder what it would be like if God were merciful but not mighty?

That He, though undeservedly kind, would be too weak to defend and too impoverished to provide? Think of the danger to us if He would be mighty but not merciful. None of us would be able to stand for another moment in the face of His appropriate wrath at our sin. But the blessed wonder of it all is that He is merciful and mighty. Willing to forgive me. Able and ready to defend and provide for me!

"Morning by morning new mercies I see!" What would a routine morning be like for you if, as Jeremiah wrote in Lamentations, His mercies were not new to us every morning? He is indeed, *"Strength for today and bright hope for tomorrow!"*

Since *"Jesus is my portion, a constant friend is He,"* I find pleasure in singing, *"Precious Lord, take my hand, Lead me on, help me stand..."* for if *"His eye is on the sparrow, I know He watches me!"*

This chapter taken from Moody *Magazine, September/October 2002*

When life is far too fast and on the verge of being out of control, it is important to "stop and smell the roses." But when you do, get beyond the refreshing elixir of the smell and the beauty. And, if they are delivered to your door, get beyond the romance. So much of what is around us, while beautiful in itself, is a reflection of the glorious creative hand of a master designer who orchestrated all of it for our pleasure and His glory. Even what we make with our own hands and conceive in our own minds is possible because we have been made in the image of a wise Creator-God. From the fountains of the deep to the frontiers of technology, He is in it all!

Look at the star-filled sky and think of Jesus. Bask in the reality that the One who formed the deep and vast universe by the word of His mouth is your Creator and Friend. See Him in the sun that rises each morning, finely tuned to neither scorch nor freeze. Catch the symbol of His hope in the early spring flower that pushes through the crusted snow.

In the Moody Video production *Planet Earth*, astronaut Colonel Guy Gardner, speaking of the marvels of creation he saw in space, pauses and, with tears welling in his eyes, says, "It's very hard to think this must have happened by chance . . . you realize at the same time that there had to be a master designer, a Creator, of this planet.

"To me, that makes life all the more special. Because that tells me that instead of me being something that just came along in the course of time to live and die, that instead of a meaningless existence, I have Someone who cares for me, who has made me and cares about me. Someone I can go to with my troubles and my cares and my joys."

You'll never feel far from God when you see Him in all that is around you.

Look for Him . . . rejoice with a grateful heart as you experience His presence.

This chapter taken from Strength for the Journey, *Moody Publishers, 2002*

S ome of you will remember when 3-D comics and movies were all the rage. To bring the picture into focus you had to wear the right eyewear— glasses composed of cardboard frames with colored cellophane lenses. Without the glasses the picture was blurry and nonsensical, but with them the picture became clear and meaningful and compellingly real. Moviegoers would scream as monsters leaped from the screen, and their stomachs would be in their throats on the roller coaster. If our whole perspective lacks an expanded point of view and is limited to this present world, then distortion will always disorient both life and faith.

Peggy Noonan, former correspondent with CBS News and speechwriter for presidents Reagan and the first George Bush, insightfully observes:

I think we have lost the old knowledge that happiness is overrated—that, in a way, life is overrated. We have lost, somehow, a sense of mystery— about us, our purpose, our meaning, our role. Our ancestors believed in two worlds, and understood this to be the solitary, poor, nasty, brutish and short one. We are the first generation of man that actually expected to find happiness here on earth, and our search for it has caused such unhappiness. The reason: If you do not believe in another, higher world, if you believe only in the flat material world around you, if you believe that this is your only chance at happiness—if that is what you believe, then you are not disappointed when the world does not give you a good measure of its riches, you are despairing. [1]

When the apostle Paul wrote that if only in this life we have faith in Christ, we are of all men most to be pitied (1 Corinthians 15:19), he was on to a very important truth. If this is the only world for us, then the misery of a passive pessimism is indeed our lot. In this statement Paul has given us a hint as to what may be wrong with our picture. Could it be that our frame of reference has been locked into this world only? The Bible indicates that there are, in fact, not two worlds as Noonan notes, but three worlds that are both real and relevant. When life with all its joys and sorrows is viewed through the broader perspectives of these other worlds, our spiritual passions reignite and our faith satisfies all unanswered questions.

Scripture crafts biblical eyewear with lenses that bring life into focus, integrating the three distinct worlds to which every believer belongs. This biblical prescription orients us to the world to come . . . the eternal world of heaven; the world within . . . the kingdom of Christ where He reigns as King over the realm of our lives and seeks to express the values, attitudes, and reactions of His kingdom through us; and the world around us . . . this present, hollow, fallen, temporal world.

⌒❧

What are the characteristics of these worlds? The world around us tends toward unfairness, danger, and disappointment, and ultimately it will leave us unsatisfied and disappointed. It is a world controlled by our adversary. Its intrinsic nature is temporal. Filled with the qualities of our good and loving God, the world to come, on the other hand, is characterized by limitless satisfaction and joy. And the redemptive world within is equipped to be a victorious, first-wave expression of our final experience in eternity. The believer is called to see all of life in the context of these three distinct spheres.

Paul Harvey's series, "The Rest of the Story," intriguingly relates real-life situations that are seemingly enigmatic and unanswerable. Then, after the final commercial break, he comes back and tells "the rest of the story." As the final details unfold, the earlier information comes into focus and makes sense. Similarly, with all three worlds in clear view, we can see life in its fullest meaning.

If all we have is this world, then revenge, bitterness, and hatred will be our response when deep injustices come upon us. If, however, we understand that this world is prone to offense and cruelty, but that in the world to come God will guarantee that every wrong will be made right and that justice will be done, we are suddenly released from the pressure of dealing with the issue ourselves. Yielding the tension to God for His care, we can be free emotionally, psychologically, and spiritually to love even our offenders. This is exactly what Paul commands that we do in Romans 12 where he says that we are not to render evil for evil, but to put wrath in its proper place. That proper place is at the throne of God who lives today in heaven and sees all that transpires on this earth. Knowing then, that God will deal from the world beyond with our enemies, we are free to respond in peace. If our enemies are hungry we can feed them, or if they're thirsty we can give them a drink (Romans 12:17–21).

Those without Christ have only this present world as their frame of reference. The world beyond is either denied or largely unnoticed. For them the world within is merely an extension of the fallen world to which they have become enslaved. That is why a life without a relationship with the King of eternity and with no confidence of a fulfilling existence in eternity is at best hollow and at worst desperate.

We of all people should be neither hollow nor desperate. Sir Fred Catherwood, a former vice president of the European Parliament who was knighted for public service, writes in an article entitled "Before It's Too Late":

> British Society has gone badly wrong. You don't just have to look at the
> terrible statistics. People have started to look back to the good old days—
> not so long ago—when the streets were safe, everyone had a job, most
> people had a home, children stayed at school, the family stayed together
> and we all looked forward to better times. We look back today because we
> dare not look forward. We live in a violent, greedy, rootless, cynical, and
> hopeless society and we don't know what's to become of it all. [2]

You might think he was writing about America. Catherwood cites causes for the decline. The first one he states is greed, which he calls "the logical result of the belief that there is not life after death. We grab what we can while we can however we can and then hold on to it hard." He goes on to note that having lost sight of the God of eternity, society is motivated by what is personally expedient. "The powerful use their power and the weak go to the wall, not just the poor, but the weak-willed, and especially all the children, who depend on the age-old disciplines and loving care of the family. As we stop believing in the dignity of man and woman made in the image of God, violence has risen dramatically." [3]

Yet, this present world often captures our attention and distracts us from our focus on the world to come and the impulses of the kingdom within, leading to disappointing consequences. In fact, most of the regrets of our lives come from failing to embrace eternity as a consuming, motivational reality and failing to align our lives to the values of the kingdom.

Greed offers us nothing more than the empty shell of things that cannot satisfy. Our preoccupation with our own advancement breeds tension, trauma, and sometimes tragedy in our most prized relationships. Our clamor for earthside power and prestige preempts the time, energy, and attention that we could give to our children, our spouses, and the less fortunate. Instead, we trade the values of the kingdom and an assured, eternal reward for a moment in the spotlight.

In hindsight, we can look back and realize that most of our lives have been poured into the bottomless bucket of this world, and that, after all is said and done, the bucket is still empty. Worse yet, imagine stepping onto the shore on the other side and realizing that we have brought nothing with us of eternal worth. Think of looking into the face of our eternal God, realizing that our lives reflect only earth-side existence rather than the meaningful, profound realities of the kingdom. In eternity our hearts may echo the words of John Greenleaf Whittier, "For of all sad words of tongue or pen, the saddest are these: 'It might have been.'"

How then do we as believers actively embrace the reality of all the worlds to which we belong? First, we learn the sequence. There are many events in life where sequence is everything. As we often say, it is important to keep first things first. It's important that national anthems be sung before games begin. That appetizers precede entrees. That engagement comes before marriage. And that crawling happens before walking. It is the same with understanding the worlds to which we belong. When embracing the reality of these worlds, sequence is everything.

Eternity is primary. Heaven must become our first and ultimate point of reference. We are built for it, redeemed for it, and on our way to it. Success demands that we see and respond to now in the light of then. All that we have, are, and accumulate must be seen as resources by which we can influence and impact the world beyond. Even our tragedies are viewed as events that can bring eternal gain.

Second, while living in light of the world to come, our lives in the here and now are to be directed by the authority of the King who lives within us. Instead of being absorbed by misdirected values and trends of this present world, we are redeemed to express the values and realities of His kingdom to the watching world around us.

Once we embrace in sequence the eternal world beyond and the eternal world within, we are ready to face the world around us realistically and triumphantly. This present world is a place created by God for His glory, His gain, and our enjoyment. But it is a place corrupted by the Fall and crowded with a fallen race. It is a place under the dominion of Satan who is bent on defacing and defaming God and His glory. The world around us is a dangerous and destructive environment that, when left to itself, creates tension and trouble.

Unfortunately, instead of a steady biblical expression of the sequence of these three elements of a believer's existence, we tend to move in and out of these worlds in a random fashion. Given the particular pressures of the moment, we periodically prioritize, ignore, forget, and reclaim their significance.

For instance, we are often pressed with the reality of eternity only when a loved one dies. Or when we grow old and begin to realize that most of life has passed and we note with regret the little we have done for eternity, the little we will take with us there, and the short time left to do much of significance for heaven's sake. Most of us live as though this world is where we are rewarded, and happiness, satisfaction, fulfillment, and prosperity not only can be ours here and now but should be.

The understanding that we have been delivered from the domain of Satan and transplanted into the kingdom of His dear Son escapes us. We seem unaware —or worse, uninterested—in the unique values of the kingdom of Christ and the fact that we are called to be an advance announcement of eternity. We remain unaware until we are confronted by a stirring sermon or perhaps a failure in life that graphically brings to light the fact that we have not responded to Him as King but have sought to manage and maneuver our own way through life for our own benefit and gain. When the sermon has faded and the failure has been reconciled, we quickly slip back into building our own kingdoms here and now.

If heaven is our consistent hope and the King is our guide and the expression of His kingdom is our calling, then life in this world comes more clearly into view. Its disappointments don't damage or surprise us. We expect little of it, for our reward is yet to come, and we hope to take captives from it into our march toward home.

In short, the blending of these worlds means that we live confidently here in the light of there, reflecting the culture and values of the kingdom within under the authority of the King.

Henry Ford, the great automobile magnate, was advised by some of his colleagues at the Ford Motor Company to hire a consultant to solve some of the problems created by the phenomenal growth of the car industry. Reluctantly, since Ford never liked to spend money, he hired a consultant by the name of Steinmetz. When Steinmetz's work was done, he sent Henry Ford a bill for $10,000—a huge sum of money in Ford's day. Ford was outraged. According to correspondence on display at the Henry Ford Museum, he wrote back to Steinmetz expressing his shock and disappointment at the cost of the consultation and requesting that Steinmetz send him a detailed invoice itemizing the details of the consultation. In this correspondence Ford said, "This is an outrageous charge for just tinkering around." Steinmetz wrote back that he was pleased to provide a detailed accounting of the cost. The itemized invoice stated $10 for tinkering around and $9,990 for knowing where to tinker.

Our problem is not that we don't spend time tinkering around with our Christianity. We have simply not known where to tinker. Knowing how to maximize our faith is not a complicated concept. It always involves the realization that we are redeemed for something far beyond ourselves, our time, our space, and our history. And that within us are planted the beginning seeds of the world to come, the indwelling King, and our commitment to the values and expressions of eternity.

Redemption has liberated us to citizenship in another world, with an insightful view of this present world and fortified by a redeemed world within. We are called to clearly view the reality of this present world, embrace the world beyond, and live by the instincts of the resurrected world within.

But not only must we see the world around us clearly, we must look far enough ahead, fully embracing the reality of the world to come.

While most all of us would like to embrace the reality of the world to come, for many it seems neither real nor relevant. The vast majority of Christians live no differently than the pagans who believe "You only go around once, so get all you can." We have somehow forgotten that heaven transforms our lives in this world. In fact, our actions become radically, wonderfully rearranged when heaven comes clearly into view. It's only when we lift our eyes to heaven that life and its faith-threatening questions take on new significance. Heaven must be more than a spiritual fantasyland, a divine Disney World in the sky. It must be our transforming point of reference.

The resurrection of Christ and His post-resurrection appearances gave the apostles a keen sense of the reality of the world to come. It was this reality that empowered, energized, and defined the New Testament church as a force with which this world could not reckon. Because heaven was real they would not be seduced by the lesser things of this world. They viewed the threat of death as simply the door to all that is better.

Having seen the reality of our world clearly and embracing the world to come leaves only a surrender to the redemptive world within to complete our reorientation. While being a Christian is a privilege that we appreciate, we often fail to accept the realities and responsibilities of the fact that the King reigns within—that we are His and He is ours, and that at our very essence we are children of His kingdom. For some reason we still live as though our lives were our own to be managed and maneuvered by our passions, pride, and the promptings of our instincts. We fail to recognize that the culture of the kingdom has been planted within our hearts and, as such, we are called to express the values, attitudes, actions, and reactions characteristic of the kingdom to come.

Refusing to live only for this present, brutish world enables us to come to grips with the transforming realities of the three worlds to which we belong. Bringing them into sync will give perspective to both pain and pleasure, gain and giving, suffering and satisfaction, heartache and happiness. It will rekindle a passion in our spirit that can sustain us just as it did the early Christians. A three-world perspective reassures us, even in the midst of pain or confusion, that God is good and life is well worth living. When we come to grips with the world around us, the world beyond us, and the world within us, we sense a revived faith, no longer quarantined by the questions of life. A three-world orientation motivates our spirits to undaunted service to Him.

A few years back, Chicago pastor Scott Willis and his wife Janet, lost six of their children in a horrific auto accident near Milwaukee. Their faith in the face of unspeakable tragedy inspired many.

In a lead editorial, the *Chicago Tribune* heralded the strength of Scott and Janet Willis's faith by quoting Scott as saying, "I must tell you, we hurt and sorrow as you parents would for your children. The depth of pain is indescribable. The Bible expresses our feelings that we sorrow, but not as those without hope." The writer of the editorial continued, "Hope is founded in faith and in the conviction, in Janet Willis's words, that 'He is the giver and the taker of life and He sustains us.'"[4] Janet and Scott are clearly in touch with the redemptive world within while aware of the short, nasty, brutish world around them. If for them life was defined by this present world alone, the devastation would have been overwhelming.

Living in and viewing all of life from other worlds, the Willises were able to transform their tragedy to His glory. Knowing that this world offers no guarantees of safety, security, and satisfaction, the Willises had cultivated an unshakable confidence in the King who lives within and ultimately brings all things to His glory. They were clearly oriented to the truth that all of life was to be seen in light of the world to come. And it was that perspective that the Willises portrayed to every major media outlet in the Midwest—a compelling victory over this present world, anchored in a firm embrace of the world to come and a full surrender to the King of the world within them.

It is this other-world point of view that prompted Scott to declare, "Janet and I have had to realize that we're not taking the short view of life. We take the long view and that includes eternal life." It's no wonder that the *Tribune* editorial concluded, "There are only two possible responses to the kind of loss that Duane [Scott] and Janet Willis suffered last week: utter despair or unquestioning faith. For the Willises, despair was never an option."[5]

This chapter taken from Eternity, *Moody Publishers, 1995*

One of the most moving scenes for me in the last movie of the epic *Lord of the Rings* trilogy was when Frodo collapsed on the very slopes of Mount Doom. So near the end of a long, long journey, with their destination at last in view, the ring bearer could go no further. With victory so close at hand in a great battle of good against evil, the forces of evil were about to win. Frodo's faithful companion, Sam, pleaded with his friend to get up and keep going—to finish the task before it was too late. When his fellow hobbit wouldn't or couldn't stir, Sam, himself exhausted beyond words, said, "Come on, Mr. Frodo, I can't carry it for you, but I can carry you." Struggling, Sam picked Frodo up and carried him to the heart of Mount Doom, where victory would finally be won.

At one time or another, each of us needs a Sam. We need someone to be there to rescue us at the brink of failure, to communicate confidence and worth in the face of impending defeat and discouragement.

When Martie and I saw *The Return of the King,* I was going through a particularly challenging time, and found myself often plagued with confusing, disheartening thoughts and feelings. Since people have this weird sense that people who do what I do don't wrestle with discouragement, I often feel deeply alone in times like these. When my heart is down, I feel that I have far more critics than champions, and I find my spirit longing for a champion to carry and wave my flag. (I know that Jesus is my champion, but there are times when you need Him to incarnate His love and care in the skin of a fellow believer.) Perhaps that's why I identified so quickly with Sam's loving willingness to carry the battle-weary Frodo.

I so desperately wanted and needed a Sam!

I had been sharing with Martie some of my internal struggle just the day before, and her input had been a great help. As we walked from the theater, I said, "I feel like I need a Sam."

She grabbed my arm and pulled me close. With delight in her eyes and voice, she said, "I'm your Sam!"

I will never forget the depth of meaning that her words and the love in her eyes had on my heart. The person who knew me and loved me more than anyone else had just pledged herself afresh to lift me up and strengthen me for the journey. Just knowing that was a wind of healing to my soul. I was not alone!

Think of what God said to Israel:

"The Lord your God carried you, just as a man carries his son, in all the way which you have walked until you came to this place . . . Even to your old age . . . I will carry you . . . and I will deliver you." *Deuteronomy 1:31; Isaiah 46:4*

Excerpted from The Final Question of Jesus © 2004 *by Dr. Joseph M. Stowell. Used by permission of Multnomah Publishers, Inc.*

SIX

TRIBUTES

Dear Joe,

As you are honored today with this book, Ruth and I want to join with your many friends in thanking you for all you mean to the Kingdom of God and to us.

God has greatly used you in your ministry at Moody Bible Institute, and for generations to come the world will continue to be impacted for Christ by those who have gone out to serve Him as a result of challenges and commitments made at Moody under your leadership. We thank God for your time at the school — He sent you there "for such a time as this."

Now as you and Martie are being led out into other areas of ministry, we pray that you will experience the richness of God's hand of blessing upon your every step as you follow Him in faith and obedience.

On a personal note, we look forward to continued fellowship with you as a member of our own Board of Directors, where we count it a privilege to have the benefit of your wisdom, insight, and prayerful participation.

With warmest Christian greetings,

—BILLY GRAHAM

Dear Joe,

My greatest claim to fame these days is that I knew Joe Stowell before he became Joe Stowell. And what a run it's been. From our earliest days as seminary students, through your years of faithful pastoral ministry, to your long tenure as Moody's seventh president, I've had the privilege of watching God mount up His blessings upon the life and ministry of my best friend. It's been a spectacle to enjoy, and none of it has surprised me.

From the start your love for Christ, for His Word and His people was plain to us all. It was what marked you then, and what has marked your ministry ever since. You are known as a wonderfully gifted communicator, a man of integrity and a seemingly tireless worker; you write as well as you preach, and many thousands have been the beneficiaries of your gifts. Yet all of these gifts are but channels. What flows through them is your devotion to the Savior, your unapologetic commitment to the Scriptures, and your infectious love for God's people. Little wonder that God has been able to bless you so.

It is sometimes said that if we can look back over our life and say we've had just one true friend, just one David to our Jonathan, then we may consider ourselves blessed. My life has been blessed with many true friends — but only one David. Like him, you too are a man after God's own heart, and a man after my heart, too.

Before the many readers of this book, let me thank God publicly for the richness of your friendship, for your fellowship in the work of the Kingdom all these years, and for your consistent model to me of what it means to be a godly man.

Your friend,

—DUANE LITFIN

My dear friend, Joe,

As the time approaches for you to step away from the role you have filled so well for almost eighteen years, I would like to add my congratulations to you along with many others who are expressing their words of commendation. All of us want you to know how very grateful we are for the faithfulness of your ministry and the fruitfulness of your leadership at Moody Bible Institute. Thank you, sincerely.

I'd like to name ten specific areas of balance I admire in your life:

- You have provided the students a good model without demanding their respect
- You have worked very hard without calling attention to the personal sacrifices
- You have remained true to the Bible without worshiping the print on its pages
- You have stayed focused on your calling without ignoring your wife and family
- You have enlarged the school's significance without building your own kingdom
- You have continued to love Christ without becoming proud of your piety
- You have built up the Body of Christ, the church, without overlooking the lost
- You have ministered far and wide without forgetting your own obedience
- You have endured your critics without becoming a cranky old codger
- You have led with distinction without losing your sense of humor

Good for you, Joe! Because God is trustworthy and full of grace, He knows better than anyone how faithfully you have invested your life these many years. Best of all, He will not forget. Your rewards will be many.

With loud applause,

—CHARLES R. SWINDOLL

Dear Joe and Martie,

I can't think of a finer pair of Christian servants and leaders than you two—I mean it! You two are THE best! When I think of you two I think of a number of qualities that are a model for millions:

- Your love for the Savior and consistent focus on Christ in all that you do.

- Your commitment to the Scripture—you have always demonstrated an unshakeable confidence in the Word of God as YOUR authority.

- Your love for God's people. I was amazed that you knew the names of EVERY student we ran into at Moody—you were bullish on the next generation of Christian soldiers!

- Your commitment to one another. You two are a team—we need more leaders like you!

- Your model of family. Not only have you two made enormous contributions to the Kingdom work, but you trained your children to do the same. And they are doing it!

- Your friendship is a great encouragement. I've never talked to you when I didn't personally benefit from your life and your words that stimulated me to love and good deeds.

- And finally your timely generosity. You two gave us a gift at a time when we really needed it. It wasn't a gift of money—it was something far more valuable—you gave us the gift of time alone together! Thank you, again.

And so, as this fruitful chapter of your lives closes, I believe this next chapter will be the best yet.

Stand firm and love the King.

—DENNIS RAINEY

Dear Joe,

I want to congratulate you on your new opportunity of ministry and to express my deep appreciation for the last eighteen years of leadership that you have given to Moody Bible Institute and the affiliated ministries as well as to the larger body of Christ worldwide. I have often commented to others, "If there ever was one born to be a general in the Christian army, Joe Stowell is a great example." Your stature, wisdom, passion, grace, and wit have been gifts of God that have been greatly used for His glory and our good.

May God continue to give you open doors and a broad platform for the proclamation of His Word and the building up of the body of Christ worldwide. We at Dallas Seminary are proud of you and take great delight in claiming you as one of our distinguished alums.

On a more personal note, Joe, thank you for the encouragement, acceptance, and model that you have been for me as a Christian leader. I've been honored by your invitations to minister alongside you on the Moody campus and in Moody conferences. I'm a better thinker and lover of our God because of the times we have spent together. Your perspective and your personal friendship have been gifts of God through you. The words of Philemon come to mind as I reflect on this last decade or two of relationship with you: "For I have come to have much joy and comfort in your love, because the hearts of the saints have been refreshed through you, brother" (Philemon 7).

May God give you and Martie and your family many years of fruitful ministry, fond memories, and an ever maturing faith. Thanks for your contribution on our campus here at Dallas. With your newfound freedom, I'm sure you can expect even more invitations to use your gifts and ministry among the DTS community. Barby and I love you and Martie.

Yours in His service,

—MARK L. BAILEY

Dear Joe,

It would take a book the size of the Encyclopedia Britannica for me to fully express the love, admiration, and respect I have for you. God has used you in my personal and ministry life in ways that only eternity will fully be able to convey. Most important, thanks for the privilege of calling you friend. I treasure the unique relationship that God has given us and look forward to seeing the next step he has in store for your life and ministry.

Joe and Martie—Lois and I love you with our lives.

—TONY EVANS

Joe,

Congratulations on eighteen years of successful leadership at Moody! Your life has added value to mine on several occasions. Your voice is fresh, your mind keen, and your life is Christlike. Blessings on your new ministry venture.

Your friend,

—JOHN MAXWELL

Dear Dr. Stowell,

One my earliest impressions of you was the way you demon-strated a genuine interest in others, fully engaging, speaking words of affirmation and encouragement, and asking questions, rather than talking about yourself. That quality, even more than your gifts and abilities, which are sizable, first gave you stature in my eyes. When I think of the times I have heard you on the platform or interacted with you personally, I think of a generous, warm-hearted man who serves the Lord with enthusiasm and joy. While you take the Lord seriously, there is nothing dour or grim about your demeanor or your communication of your faith. Your infectious passion and winsome spirit draw those around you to the Christ you love. I pray it will always be so and that the Lord will keep you and Martie faithful and fervent in the race—all the way to the finish line!

—NANCY LEIGH DeMOSS

Dear Joe,

Esther won a beauty contest to become queen. You will probably never win a beauty contest, but you have something much bigger in common with the Jewish girl who rescued her people—you were clearly brought to your position at Moody "for such a time as this."

You have embodied things that are the essence of Moody Bible Institute—a deep love affair with God's Word, an unswerving loyalty to God's Word, a contagious passion for the work of Christ on Planet Earth. While I'm privileged as you are to be a messenger of the greatest message in the world, I personally love to listen to you. Your unique ability to bring the truth to life, your winsome vulnerability, and your passionate personality are powerful tools in the Master's hands. You are, through God's Spirit, a magnet for God.

Seasons change—as they are for you and for Moody now. I have full confidence that for both you and Moody—in the oft-repeated mantra of Torrey Johnson—"in Jesus, the best is always yet to come." Thank you for touching my life and for providing exemplary Christian leadership.

Very grateful for you,

—RON HUTCHCRAFT

Dear Joseph,

I want to be one of the many to thank you and congratulate you for your God-blessed ministry.

Joe, God has graced you with a great mind, a deep spirit, and a firm and a quiet personality that make you easy to be around. Our people at Bellevue Baptist Church were greatly blessed when you ministered to us. I love and respect you and so do the people of Bellevue.

It is not an exaggeration to say that your ministry has impacted America and the world.

Thank you for the privilege of letting me call you friend.

I believe that your future is bright and resplendent with the power of God.

God is love. Jesus is wonderful.

In His dear name,

—ADRIAN ROGERS

My dear Joe,

One of the greatest blessings in my life was the day I got to meet you during the Olympics in Atlanta and the friendship that has developed since then.

I am so honored to call you and Martie friends and co-laborers for Christ. God has used you to bless so many people . . . and I believe the best is yet to come.

I look forward to many years of close partnership in the ministry. Your friend,

—MICHAEL YOUSSEF

Dear Joe,

My thoughts and prayers are with you as you transition from giving leadership to Moody Bible Institute to your new ministry outreach. You will be greatly missed at Moody. We trust the Lord will strengthen you and renew your vision as you begin this new chapter in your life.

You are an inspiration to multiple thousands of people around the world. Thank you for your example, for your commitment to dynamically preaching the Gospel, and effectively teaching God's Word. The Lord has gifted you in remarkable ways and I look forward to seeing what is in store for you as you continue to serve Him faithfully.

God bless you.

Your friend,

—FRANKLIN GRAHAM

Dear Joseph,

I thank God for you and for your faithfulness to Christ and for your steadfastness in ministry during your eighteen-year tenure at Moody Bible Institute. But most of all, I praise God for the way you have magnified Jesus, especially in these recent years. Oh how infinitely worthy the Lord of the universe is to be trusted and loved and followed and treasured above all things. You have modeled that for us, and you have written well about it.

The legacy you leave will be durable, both institutionally and spiritually, because Christ has been at the center. As you take up a new challenge, my prayer is that more and more you will magnify Christ in your body, whether by life or by death.

It has been an honor to watch the grace of God triumph in you and through you during these years. I praise Him with you for this wonderful work.

Your friend and partner in the great work,

—JOHN PIPER

It was my privilege to be a member of the Moody Board of Trustees at the time Joe Stowell was selected for the presidency. There were a number of formidable men on the list of those to be considered. But in our minds, Dr. Stowell stood out among them for his unique heritage and giftedness. It was also evident in his prior ministry that God had His hand on him in a powerful way. We are all aware now of how strategic and Spirit-led that decision was.

I rejoice in the way the Lord has used Joe in these years at Moody to sustain the biblical commitment and to enlarge the influence of this great institute. Thank you, Joe, for your continued faithfulness—a legacy worthy of honor that will not be forgotten.

—JOHN MACARTHUR

Joe Stowell, who is one of my closest friends, has been a great leader of Moody, faithfully carrying on the great heritage of that institution. No one, in my opinion, preaches more soundly and more effectively than Joe Stowell; I pray as he takes on his new assignment there will be even more opportunities for his voice to be heard in the broad evangelical community. Count me a charter member of the Joe Stowell fan club. I thank the Lord He has raised Joe and Martie up for the wonderful witness they are, and for the great leadership he provides not only for Moody, but for evangelicals at large. Well done, Joe!

—CHARLES COLSON

One of the great joys and privileges of my life is to know Joe Stowell! We have known each other for more than fifteen years. I have had the honor of ministering alongside him at conferences and events as well as sharing personal moments of wonderful fellowship and prayer. Joe is a model of godliness, consistency, and integrity. What you see on a platform or hear on the radio is what you get in private when you're up close and personal.

You can't help but be drawn to Joe Stowell. He embodies that rather unusual combination of outstanding leadership gifts and abilities, being a compelling preacher of the gospel as well as having a great capacity for relationships. He is a generous, kingdom-oriented leader who is full of compassion and kindness. He is an open, inviting, gracious man who loves to promote others. It's no wonder that he is becoming one of the church's leading statesmen in our generation.

I love and appreciate this dear brother. When I call him my friend, I boast. When he calls me his friend I am greatly humbled!

—CRAWFORD W. LORITTS, JR.

High on my list of respected friends is Joe Stowell. He invigorates and re-calibrates me. He is a walking tandem of prophet and pastor; visionary and manager; professor and preacher. This guy is no ordinary Joe. I'm honored to call him brother.

—MAX LUCADO

Dr. Stowell is a man of many talents. But what I admire most is his heart: sensitive, generous, and ever caring. All who know him agree that his passion to be like Jesus is the core of his motivation and ministry.

—ERWIN W. LUTZER

It was a chilly Easter morning and thousands of British evangelicals were gathered in the large circus tent to hear the closing address of the week. It had been a good week, but why was it to be concluded by an American? That was the question being asked by many. Or it was until he stood up to speak.

Because that calm, clear voice of Joe (with Martie praying as usual behind him) rang out loud and clear.

He spoke of going home, not to places of temporary residence but to heaven. Few missed the point, or remained unmoved, all knew the American had hit a home run that morning! It was fantastic ministry, but then that is Joseph Stowell!

He and Martie have been friends, mentors, and models to so many—Ruth and I just feel honored and privileged to count ourselves in that very large band who on this occasion would simply wish to breathe a profound "thank you" for all that they have allowed the Lord to do through them—in the USA and around the world.

Their many acts of kindness and wisdom and grace have shown that the knowledge of the principles of heaven has not been relegated to hearsay or mere anticipation of the future. It has been a message both lived and spoken. And will be hopefully for many years ahead. Meanwhile, so many will be grateful.

With warmest greetings,

—CLIVE CALVER

As an alumnus of Moody Bible Institute, I have often prayed for God's continued blessing upon the school that D. L. Moody founded. One of the greatest of those blessings was God's hand in bringing Dr. Joseph Stowell to serve as president. For the past eighteen years, God has used Dr. Stowell to guide the institute through the troubled waters of contemporary culture. With humility and strength he has stood firmly upon the foundation of God's Word, while seeking ways to communicate timeless truth into a changing culture. He has led the school to take advantage of the advances of technology to expand the ministry of the institute into a global training center.

While relating to the faculty and staff as a servant-leader, he has also taken time to get to know students and give personal encouragement. His approachability, and openness to the ideas of students, faculty, and friends, while at the same time keeping his ears open to the voice of God, has made him a unique leader. I've read his books, listened to his sermons, observed his life, and in so doing my own life and ministry have been greatly enriched. For that I am eternally thankful.

—GARY D. CHAPMAN

I count it an extreme privilege and honor to be extended the opportunity to express my admiration and respect for Dr. Joseph Stowell. Joe has had extraordinary influence in my life and a number of the most important decisions that I have made. His influence extends not only to my thinking about theological issues but my family, children, and marriage. I have jokingly told him on numerous occasions that, "Someday when I grow up I want to be like you." Though only my senior by about ten years, his wisdom, integrity, and leadership under immense pressure and responsibility are that which I aspire to in my own walk with God and ministry of the gospel. Joe, thank you for who you are and what you have allowed Christ to accomplish through you by His grace. Your focus on Jesus has left an indelible print upon my heart, life, and ministry.

—Chip Ingram

Dr. Joseph Stowell has served with distinction as the president of the Moody Bible Institute. Furthermore, he has brought honor to his Lord Jesus Christ as a Christian statesman, who served all of God's people. Everyone in Dr. Stowell's realm of influence is important. While rubbing shoulders with the best-known Christian leaders, Joe always remembered to engage the waitress, the waiter, and any of the service staff. He always remembers the "little people." Once, stepping into an MBI elevator a petite custodial lady was struggling to clean the tall elevator doors. But the height of the doors was way beyond her reach. Joe, towering over the little lady, grabbed a rag and helped her finish her job. That's Joe, fully competent among the greats and totally compassionate among the modest.

Once Joe and I walked the halls of MBI and one of the cafeteria workers looked up with a smile as Joe called his name and made an inside joke that evoked a beaming grin from the worker. He engaged students, alumni, faculty and staff with the energy of a seasoned ambassador. When he enters a room filled with the best of the Kingdom of God, Joe is constantly drawing in the shy, the quiet, the reserved to engage everyone. He encourages the discouraged, he uplifts the weary, he promotes others over himself and he serves with pristine humility. Well done, Dr. Stowell! You have blessed so many of us and we are all further along in our service of the King because you cheered us on.

Eager for HIS Return!

—BRUCE W. FONG

"Therefore, my dear brothers, stand firm. Let nothing move you. Always give yourselves fully to the work of the Lord because you know that your labor in the Lord is not in vain."

—1 Corinthians 15:58

Dr. Joseph Stowell is one of God's choice servants. He has provided exceptional leadership for the Moody Bible Institute over the past eighteen years. Beyond his ministry at Moody, Joe is one of the few leaders who has made a significant mark on the kingdom throughout the world by way of his books, articles, and excellent teaching and preaching.

Our Lord has made Joe and Martie a model for Christian couples with their deep love for each other, their family, and God's family.

Pat and I wish them well in their new ministry which, no doubt, will continue to have God's hand upon it. We rejoice that they are graduates of Cedarville University.

—PAUL DIXON

How does anyone estimate the impact of an eighteen-year ministry at an institution such as the Moody Bible Institute? During those eighteen years, Dr. Joseph Stowell has impacted the lives of countless hundreds of students, literally thousands of visitors to the Moody Bible Institute, to say nothing of his influence with the faculty he has so ably led.

But, of course, beyond any shadow of a doubt, the students who have traversed the halls of Moody that have had the opportunity to observe the consistency of his life, the brilliance of his messages, and the emphasis of his heart know that these are the places where the real accounting will occur in the years that lie ahead. Moody graduates who have been blessed by his ministry will be found in all the mission extensions around the earth to say nothing of the pulpits of the churches in America, and each one will have something of the stamp of the life and ministry of Joseph Stowell upon his heart. No wonder that all of us gather together today in thanking God for the impact of this remarkable man.

—PAIGE PATTERSON

Dr. Joseph Stowell is one of the evangelical world's great leaders, combining a passionate vision with authentic leadership and deep theological conviction. In a day of diminished Christian influence and diverse challenges, Joe Stowell has offered a steady hand, guiding the Moody Bible Institute through strategic years of growth and opportunity, and expanding his influence throughout the larger evangelical world.

Throughout his ministry, Joe Stowell has combined the heart of a pastor with the mind of a strategic thinker and the instinct of a true leader. He has addressed the cultural issues of our day with a clear word of Christian conviction, even as he has raised up a generation of Christian leaders who are now spread all over the world as pastors, missionaries, evangelists, and dedicated laypersons.

We all stand in Joe Stowell's debt, even as we are encouraged by his example. Furthermore, we will continue to expect great things from Joe Stowell so long as he lives. He will not let us down.

—R. ALBERT MOHLER, JR.

About Joseph Stowell

DR. JOSEPH STOWELL served from 1987 to 2005 as the seventh president of Moody Bible Institute. His prevailing passions have been to express the heart of the gospel by keeping Christ and His saving work preeminent in all that Moody endeavors to do; to embrace all of the body of Christ across color and class distinctions; and to focus attention on ministry needs in the urban centers, as well as on global needs and trends. Under his leadership MBI ministries, physical facilities, and academic offerings expanded significantly. His love for students and belief in their capacity to make a difference for Christ has been a hallmark of his presidency.

In 2004 Dr. Stowell received the Evangelical Christian Publishers Association Gold Medallion Award for his Moody Publishers title *The Trouble with Jesus.* He is the author of numerous books, including *Why It's Hard to Love Jesus, Perilous Pursuits, Shepherding the Church, Eternity, Coming Home, Strength for the Journey, The Dawn's Early Light, Fan the Flame, Kingdom Conflict, The Weight of Your Words,* and *The Upside of Down* (all Moody Publishers), as well as *Following Christ* (Zondervan), *Simply Jesus,* and *The Final Question of Jesus* (both Multnomah). For many years he was a popular columnist for *Moody* magazine. Dr. Stowell has connected personally with listeners on more than 400 stations through the award-winning radio ministry of *Proclaim!* He speaks and teaches at conferences worldwide.

Son and grandson of pastors, Dr. Stowell is a graduate of Cedarville University and Dallas Theological Seminary and was honored with a doctor of divinity degree from The Master's College in 1987. After graduating from seminary, Dr. Stowell served as senior pastor of churches in Ohio, Indiana, and Michigan for sixteen years prior to coming to MBI.

Subsequent to leaving Moody, Dr. Stowell is beginning a new chapter as teaching pastor at Harvest Bible Chapel in Rolling Meadows, Illinois, in suburban Chicago. He and his wife, Martie, are the parents of three grown children.

Notes

CHAPTER SIX: WHAT IT MEANS TO FOLLOW

1. St. Augustine, Sermon #48, Micah 6:8.

CHAPTER SEVEN: RIGHTEOUS RELIGION—OR RADICAL REDEMPTION?

1. James McBride, *The Color of Water: A Black Man's Tribute to His White Mother* (New York: Putnam/Riverhead, 1996), 42–43.
2. Ibid., 165.
3. Ibid., 50.

CHAPTER EIGHT: LIFE AMONG THE FORGIVEN MUCH

1. James McBride, *The Color of Water: A Black Man's Tribute to His White Mother* (New York: Putnam/Riverhead, 1996), 217.

CHAPTER FIFTEEN: OUR SEARCH FOR SIGNIFICANCE

1. R. C. Sproul, *The Hunger for Significance* (Ventura, Calif.: Regal, 1993), 21.

CHAPTER SIXTEEN: REDEEMING PRIDE

1. C. S. Lewis, *A Mind Awake: An Anthology of C. S. Lewis,* ed. Clyde S. Kilby (New York: Harvest, 1968), 115.

CHAPTER EIGHTEEN: FLAVORING OUR WORLD—FOR HIM

1. Interview, Lisa Beamer and Larry King, *Larry King Live!* 18 September 2001.
2. In John MacArthur Jr, *MacArthur New Testament Commentary Series: Matthew 1–7* (Chicago: Moody, 1985), 242.
3. H.L. Mencken, *The Minority Report: H.L. Mencken's Notebooks* (New York: Knopf, 1956), no. 309.
4. Speech of Mother Teresa of Calcutta to the National Prayer Breakfast, Washington, D.C., 3 February 1994. This text was accessed at www.priestsforlife.org in the subsection Brochures.
5. Philo, *De Specialibus Legibus,* 2:253, quoted in N.T. Wright, *The Challenge of Jesus* (London: SPCA, 2000), 379.
6. N. T. Wright, *The Challenge of Jesus,* 38.

CHAPTER NINETEEN: SHOWING UP FOR HIM

1. Charles Colson, "Reaching the Pagan Mind," *Christianity Today*, 9 November 1992, 112, quoted in Gene Edward Veith Jr., *Postmodern Times: A Christian Guide to Contemporary Thought and Culture* (Wheaton, Ill.: Crossway, 1994), 15–16.

2. David McCullough, *Truman* (New York: Simon & Schuster, 1992), 185.

3. Ibid.

4. Vincent Carroll and David Shiflett, *Christianity on Trial: Arguments Against Anti-Religious Bigotry* (San Francisco: Encounter, 2001), 139.

5. Carl F. Henry, *Twilight of a Great Civilization: The Drift Toward Neo-Paganism* (Wheaton, Ill.: Crossway, 1988), 18–19.

CHAPTER TWENTY-THREE: IN OTHER WORLDS

1. Peggy Noonan, "You'd Cry Too," *Forbes*, 14 September 1992, 65.

2. Fred Catherwood, "Before It's Too Late," *Evangelicals Now;* as quoted in J. I. Packer, "Fear of Looking Forward," *Christianity Today*, 12 December 1994, 13.

3. Ibid.

4. "Sustained in a Tragedy by Faith," *Chicago Tribune*, 18 November 1994, 1:18.

5. Michael A. Lev, "Couple Held on to God in Tragedy," *Chicago Tribune*, 17 November 1994, 1:1, 18.

SINCE 1894, Moody Publishers has been dedicated to equip and motivate people to advance the cause of Christ by publishing evangelical Christian literature and other media for all ages, around the world. Because we are a ministry of the Moody Bible Institute of Chicago, a portion of the proceeds from the sale of this book go to train the next generation of Christian leaders.

If we may serve you in any way in your spiritual journey toward understanding Christ and the Christian life, please contact us at www.moodypublishers.com.

"All Scripture is God-breathed and is useful for teaching, rebuking, correcting and training in righteousness, so that the man of God may be thoroughly equipped for every good work."
—*2 TIMOTHY 3:16, 17*

MOODY
PUBLISHERS

THE NAME YOU CAN TRUST®

I WOULD FOLLOW JESUS TEAM

SENIOR PROJECT EDITOR
Elizabeth Cody Newenhuyse

COVER DESIGN
Smartt Guys

INTERIOR DESIGN
BlueFrog Design

PRINTING AND BINDING
Lake Book Manufacturing, Inc.

The typeface for the text of this book is
Fournier MT